T0110945

Designed FOR PLEASURES

SAMUEL SEGUN OLADIPO

WESTBOW
PRESS®
A DIVISION OF THOMAS NELSON
& ZONDERVAN

Copyright © 2021 Samuel Segun Oladipo.

All rights reserved. No part of this book may be used or reproduced by any means, graphic, electronic, or mechanical, including photocopying, recording, taping or by any information storage retrieval system without the written permission of the author except in the case of brief quotations embodied in critical articles and reviews.

WestBow Press books may be ordered through booksellers or by contacting:

WestBow Press
A Division of Thomas Nelson & Zondervan
1663 Liberty Drive
Bloomington, IN 47403
www.westbowpress.com
844-714-3454

Because of the dynamic nature of the Internet, any web addresses or links contained in this book may have changed since publication and may no longer be valid. The views expressed in this work are solely those of the author and do not necessarily reflect the views of the publisher, and the publisher hereby disclaims any responsibility for them.

Any people depicted in stock imagery provided by Getty Images are models, and such images are being used for illustrative purposes only.
Certain stock imagery © Getty Images.

Scripture taken from the King James Version of the Bible.

Scripture taken from the New King James Version. Copyright © 1979, 1980, 1982 by Thomas Nelson, Inc. Used by permission. All rights reserved.

Scripture quotations are from The Holy Bible, English Standard Version® (ESV®), copyright © 2001 by Crossway, a publishing ministry of Good News Publishers. Used by permission. All rights reserved.

ISBN: 978-1-6642-1715-7 (sc)
ISBN: 978-1-6642-1717-1 (hc)
ISBN: 978-1-6642-1716-4 (e)

Library of Congress Control Number: 2020925392

Print information available on the last page.

WestBow Press rev. date: 01/07/2021

Contents

This book is dedicated to all creatures of God, visible and invisible. All creatures deserve adequate attention as much as the Creator gives to them.

—S. S. Oladipo

Acknowledgements

First of all, I will like to appreciate my heavenly Father, my Lord and Savior Jesus Christ, and my Inspiration, The Holy Spirit-for without them I could do nothing.

I am very grateful to my loving and dedicated wife, Oluwakemi and my beloved children, Ibukunoluwa, Ifeoluwa and Temiloluwa who helped in one way or another to making the writing and puplication of this book a reality.

Special gratitude to all my spiritual Fathers: Pastor W.F. Kumuyi, Pastor Thomson Aderemi and countless others, co-ministers, church members and friends for their love, prayers and motivations.

Finally, I will love to express my profound gratitude to the entire staff of WestBowPress whose warmth, labor and support encourged the publication of this book.

Introduction

Thou art worthy, O Lord, to receive glory and honor and power: for thou hast created *all things*, and for thy *pleasure* they are and were created. (Revelation 4:11, emphasis added)

Everything visible or invisible; everything in motion or motionless; everything in the heavens, on earth, or beneath the earth; everything in God or through God; everything in their original state and final state—they were all meant and designed for pleasures. Everything, in diverse state of all beings from whatever beginnings, whatever shape, color, outlook, however small or great, high or low, broad or narrow, thin—you name it, was all designed for pleasures. One of the most fascinating things about God, the Creator of all things, is that He is a God of pleasures. The motive behind everything He created is pleasure! God is pleasured by whatever He is engaged in. His motives and motivations are borne out of pleasures. The summations of all things God made is found in Revelation 4:11. All things, both great and small. All things without exception. All things visible to God, who can see all things. All things visible or invisible to human eyes. All things in heaven, on earth, underneath the earth, or on other planets.

All things can be said to be pleasurable originally, because there was never evil in the original creation! The original state had no iota of evil thing, visible or invisible. The originator of the idea of creation had no evil in Him, and neither could He ever imagine creating any singular thing to represent evil. Therefore, there was no evil thought, evil plan, or evil stuff at any state or realm. All creation must have been by all means designed for pleasure. It is worthy of note that from the account of Genesis that:

> Nothing was originally meant or made for sorrow.
> Nothing was originally meant or created for death.
> Nothing was originally created for sickness.
> Nothing was originally created for anguish.
> Nothing was originally created for anything close to hell or the like. (In fact, hell was not in the agenda of the Creator.)
> Nothing was originally created for slavery.
> Nothing was originally created for lack.
> Nothing was originally created for war.
> Nothing was originally created for oppression.
> Nothing was originally created for depression.
> Nothing was originally created for displeasure.
> Nothing was originally created for regrets.
> Nothing was originally created for punishment.
> Nothing was originally created for misery.
> Nothing was originally created for rigor.
> Nothing was originally created for rancor.
> Nothing was originally created for suffering.
> Nothing was originally created for any form of abuse.
> Nothing was originally created to intimidate.
> Nothing was originally created to suppress.
> Nothing was originally created for conflicts.

Even Satan, the embodiment of all evils, was not originally created with any spot of evil, as portrayed in Ezekiel 28:13–15.

> Thou hast been in Eden the garden of God; every precious stone was thy covering, the sardius, topaz, and the diamond, the beryl, the onyx, and the jasper, the sapphire, the emerald, and the carbuncle, and gold: the workmanship of thy tabrets and of thy pipes was prepared in thee in the day that thou wast created.

Thou art the anointed cherub that covereth; and I have set thee so: thou wast upon the holy mountain of God; thou hast walked up and down in the midst of the stones of fire. Thou wast perfect in thy ways from the day that thou wast created, till iniquity was found in thee.

Little wonder that in His earthly ministry, Jesus Christ made an emphatic statement about the state of things in respect to the issue of marriage, being the Creator's first institution on earth. "In the beginning it was not so" (Matthew 19:8).

He could have said the same of practically every other thing.
He could have said the same about the relationship between men and their neighbors.
He could have said the same of humans and animals.
He could have said the same of the ecosystem.
He could have said the same of the relationship between God and man.
He could have said the same about the economy and social lives.
He could have said the same of the rule of laws.
He could have said the same of natural resources.
He could have said the same of systems of this world.
He could have said the same of changes in times and seasons.
He could have said the same of religious believes.
He could have said the same of countless number of things.
In fact, he saw all men as wanderers—like sheep without shepherds.

Anything or broadly speaking, everything that ever came from God, was absolutely good and created for all good purposes. No one ever knew God as much as Jesus Christ.

The picture painted of God and His ultimate character is through the lips of the one who knows Him more than any angel or any known prophet in the person of Jesus Christ, His only begotten Son. "And he said unto them, why callest thou me good? There is none good but one, that is, God" (Matthew 19:17). Whatever comes from Him has to be within Him, for the Son of God also said in Luke 6:45, "A good man out of the good treasure of his heart brings forth good; (something pleasurable, something admirable) and an evil man out of the evil treasure of his heart brings forth evil. For out of the abundance of the heart [everything God created came out of the abundance of His heart] his mouth speaks."

Humanly speaking, even though it's practically impossible to know all the creation of God in its entirety, the fact remains that because the Creator of all things created for His pleasures, and God is not only good but love (1 John 4:7–8) "beloved, let us love one another; for love is of God; for every one that loveth is born of God, and knoweth God. He that loveth not knoweth not God: for GOD IS LOVE." The pleasure of God is at the very core of the manifestations of all He has created in the heavens, on the earth, or below the earth, as buttressed in Ecclesiastes 3:11, "He hath made *everything beautiful in His time* [anything beautiful attracts pleasure, delight] also He hath set the world in their heart, so that no man can find out the work that God maketh from the beginning to the end" (emphasis added).

There is a common adage that God's time is the best. It is not out of place that it was when God decided to create things, they came out of Him. All that He created was His exclusive idea, and the timing was not anyone's dictation. Whatever idea He had was excellent because none is as excellent as God. If it is therefore true to the word that He made all things beautiful in his time, then all that He made was beautiful and designed for pleasures.

God's ultimate pleasure in His creature is clearly affirmed in Genesis, the book of the beginning of things, and in the book of Job. Genesis 1:28 says, "And God blessed them, and God said unto them, Be fruitful, and multiply, and replenish the earth, and subdue it: and have dominion over the fish of the sea, and over the fowl of the air, and over every living thing that moveth upon the earth." In other words, all things were made available for the pleasure of humankind in His domain. The Creator Himself rejoiced because He was pleasured by the work of His hands when He exclaimed with delight in Genesis 1:31, "And God saw everything that he had made, and, behold, it was very good. And the evening and the morning were the sixth day." Can a good God rejoice and make such a delightful shout of contentment and satisfaction in what was not pleasurable?

Can a perfect God rejoice over anything and express such in clear terms for all to hear, except it achieves a goal of excellence?

Can a praise loving God sort of draw the attention of multitudes to a shameful and ridiculous event, except if it was glorious and worthy of praises?

Can the God of all wisdom approve a failure and say He is wise and almighty?

Can He say after the creation that there is none like Him, except He is a perfectionist to the core?

Can God who is all in all brag on nothing in this manner?

> To whom then will ye liken me, or shall I be equal? saith the Holy One. Lift up your eyes on high, and behold who hath created these things, that bringeth out their host by number: he calleth them all by names by the greatness of his might, for that he is strong in power; not one faileth. (Isaiah 40:25–26 KJV)

In Job 36:11, God emphatically promises, "If they obey and serve him, they shall spend *their days* in prosperity, and their *years* in *pleasures*" (emphasis added), ultimately showing the very desire and purpose of God in and for all creatures.

Nothing that has no good pleasure ever originated from God, hence the original motive of God in whatsoever He created was pleasure and for the pleasure of whom He originally bestowed them at any given time. When all is said and done, at the consummation of all things, when there shall be the emergence of the new heaven and a new Earth, His purpose and desire will still have the original label and signature "Thou art worthy, O Lord, to receive glory and honor and power: for thou hast created all things, and for thy pleasure they are and were created," which will ultimately be to the pleasure and delight of all things with the Creator and that will be for all eternity.

It's quite fascinating how the Psalmist surveyed the handiwork of God in Psalm 8.

> O LORD our Lord, how excellent is thy name in all
> the earth!
> Who hast set thy glory above the heavens?
> Out of the mouth of babes and sucklings hast thou
> ordained strength because of thine enemies,
> That thou mightest still the enemy and the avenger.
> When I consider thy heavens, the work of thy fingers,
> The moon and the stars, which thou hast ordained;
> What is man, that thou art mindful of him?
> And the son of man, that thou visitest him?
> For thou hast made him a little lower than the angels,
> And hast crowned him with glory and honour.
> Thou madest him to have dominion over the works of
> thy hands;
> Thou hast put all things under his feet:
> All sheep and oxen,
> Yea, and the beasts of the field;
> The fowl of the air, and the fish of the sea,
> And whatsoever passeth through the paths of the seas.
> O LORD our Lord,
> How excellent is thy name in all the earth!

One

—— ∽ ——

THE CREATION OF ALL THINGS
AND FOR WHAT PURPOSE?

The Bible, the most authoritative source of the origin and originator of all creation, states, "In the beginning God created the heaven and the earth" (Genesis 1:1). However, at a point in time, the things that contradicted pleasure to the Creator were clearly pointed out: "And the earth was without form, and void; and darkness was upon the face of the deep." Without form, void, and darkness—all these made a gloomy, disastrous, and unpleasant picture, which did not please God. This brought about a swift reaction from the Creator in order to bring about His original intended design. "And the Spirit of God moved upon the face of the waters. And God said let there be light."(Genesis 1:2b) The moment light appeared, you could feel the ecstatic pleasure of God revealed by the fact that "God saw the light, that it was good."(Genesis 1:4a). Imagine how wonderful the Creator must have felt while admiring the light, a significant milestone in the project He set out to accomplish. The angels around Him must have felt the same, rejoicing in the handiwork of the almighty God. It was something new, something great and fascinating.

The Creator must have been so pleased that the summary of His delight was expressed in the fact that it was good. Good things are meant to pleasure in manifold degrees. And so light shining in darkness was certainly a source of great delight and pleasure to all who witnessed this new thing. It is needful to say that great achievements bring delights and motivation to make more progress. Hence, the Creator was sort of motivated by the pleasantness and fulfillment in the creation of the light to take another step forward.

"And God divided the light from the darkness."(Genesis 1:4b). Notice the beautiful scenario in respect to what came out of God's thoughts. Psalm 145:9 says, "The LORD is good to *all*: and his tender mercies are over *all his works*" (emphasis added). "And Jeremiah records God's thought: "For I know the thoughts that I think toward you, says the LORD, thoughts of peace, and not of evil, to give you an expected end" (Jeremiah 32:11).

The swiftness in the move of the Spirit of God seems to suggest that the Creator was highly displeased with the way things were before the manifestation of the light. The pleasures of God were not satisfied.

> Thou wilt shew me the path of life: in thy presence is fullness of joy; at thy right hand there are pleasures for evermore. (Psalm 16:11)
> Now the Lord is that Spirit: and where the Spirit of the Lord is, there is liberty. (2 Corinthians 3:17)

God, being a God of pleasures, had displeasure for the darkness, the void, bondage, and other negativities. He would not have that without effecting a drastic change to the unpleasant gloom. For this reason, He moved to rearrange things as originally intended to satisfy his desires. Hence the proclamation "And God said, Let there be light: and there was light. And God saw the light, that it was good."(Genesis 1:3-4a). You could almost read the jubilant mind of God with the result that came out of the decree He issued out.

Why light? Anywhere there is light, gloom disappears, darkness departs, sadness departs, confusion departs, unpleasantness departs, uncertainty disappears, and gloominess vanishes. There was no doubt that the pleasure of God was satisfied with the affirmation of the fact that when God saw the light, it sort of wooed Him that He could not hide His feelings about the result. He immediately made a declaration to confirm His pleasure and delight that it was good. Good things delight, good things please, and good things cause joy, happiness, and the motivation or desire for even more. It must be noted that God Himself is referred to as light.

The ultimate pleasures of the Creator are expressly and strongly outlined in James 1:17, which says, "Every good gift and every perfect gift is from above, and cometh down from the Father of lights, with whom is no variables, neither shadow of turning." What a delightful scripture worthy of note that every good and perfect gift comes from the Father of light. What could be more pleasurable than good things and good gifts? All good things or gifts are designed for the pleasure of both the giver and the receiver. God has only good things to give because He is good and has nothing evil. Therefore, He delights to give what He has just to make whoever receives it richly enjoy it and give glory to Him in return. Whatever comes from God is so good that the receiver cannot but broadcast it to others—like the psalmist who says, "Oh taste and see that Lord is good" (Psalm 34:8). A taste of goodness is a taste of good feelings and pleasure. You want more of what is good and pleasant. You want more of God, who gives only what is good.

Jesus Christ, the Son of God, is referred to primarily as light. He is the perfect representative of God the Father. "I am the light of the world: he that followeth me shall not walk in darkness, but shall have the light of life" (John 8:12).

This same light of the world says, "The thief cometh not but for to steal, and to kill and to destroy: I am come that they might have life, and that they might have it more abundantly" (John 10:10).

Abundant life is a design of everything good, everything lovely, everything healthy, and everything rich, joyful, and happy—it is life in its fullness, holy life, fulfilled life, jubilant life, and resourceful life. This proclamation of Jesus Christ in His earthly ministry was centered on nothing but a promise to restore God's original plan before sin came into the world. This is also brought about primarily by the means of the light. It is therefore not a coincidence that the creation of light preceded other creatures—it was symbolic.

After the appearance of the light, subsequent creations were made, and each enjoyed the delight and pleasures of God. Things that are done in order normally attract much delight, and hence much pleasures.

Things done in order look beautiful and are pleasurable to behold.

Things done in order stimulate the senses.

Things that are done in order inspire.

Things that are done in order are products of excellence.

Things that are done in order are thoughtfully executed.

Things that are done in order are manifestations of a deliberate effort.

Things that are done in order are meant to attract adoration.

Things that are done in order usually attract inquisitiveness.

The end product of things done in order is decency and a product of pleasure.

It is always the delight of God that "all things be done decently and in order" (1 Corinthians 14:40).

Eventually, the Creator took His pleasure and desires to the highest level in Genesis 1:26–31.

> And God said, "Let us make man in our image, after our likeness: and let them have dominion over the fish of the sea, and over the fowl of the air, and over the cattle, and over all the earth, and over every creeping thing that creepeth upon the earth." So God created man in his own image, in the image of God created he him; male and female created he them. And God blessed them, and God said unto them, "be fruitful, and multiply, and replenish the earth, and subdue it: and have dominion over the fish of the sea, and over the fowl of the air, and over every living thing that moveth upon the earth." And his pleasure was fulfilled in that it is said that "And God saw *everything that he had made, and, behold, it was very good.* And the evening and the morning were the sixth day." (emphasis added)

Many things stand out here to show the pleasures of God—the creation of humans in His likeness. It is a pointer to the fact that God has pleasure in Himself. Ephesians 5:29 says, "For no man ever yet hated his own flesh; but nourisheth and cherisheth it." Hence the Creator has pleasure in Himself as much as He has pleasure in His creation. For this reason, He blessed all that He created. Who is it that pronounces a blessing on what does not give one pleasure, joy, satisfaction, glory, and delight? He also decreed on them to multiply. No one ever wants a multiplication of that which brings agony, pain, and disaster. Little wonder, then, when later on, there was a mess in the original creation, and God's pleasures were withdrawn.

> "And the LORD God said unto the serpent, Because thou hast done this, thou art cursed above all cattle, and above every beast of the field; upon thy belly shalt thou go, and dust shalt thou eat all the days of thy life. (Genesis 3:14).

> Unto the woman he said, I will greatly multiply thy sorrow and thy conception; in sorrow thou shalt bring forth children. (Genesis 3:16a).

> And unto Adam he said, "Because thou hast hearkened unto the voice of thy wife, and hast eaten of the tree, of which I commanded thee, saying, Thou shalt not eat of it: cursed is the ground for thy sake; in sorrow shalt thou eat of it all the days of thy life; Thorns also and thistles shall it bring forth to thee; and thou shalt eat the herb of the field;·In the sweat of thy face shalt thou eat bread, till thou return unto the ground; for out of it wast thou taken: for dust thou art, and unto dust shalt thou return." (Genesis 3:17).

The displeasure of the Creator ultimately brought about death that was not originally intended!

The prayers of Jesus Christ, the Son of God, in Matthew 6:9–10 showcase the pleasure of God in respect to His creations in heaven and on earth. "After this manner therefore pray ye: Our Father which art in heaven, Hallowed be thy name. Thy kingdom come, *Thy will be done in earth, as it is in heaven*" (emphasis added). His will, His motives, and His desires are His pleasures. It was originally intended that as heaven is filled with His pleasures, so should it be in everything He has created. Whatever or wherever His kingdom extends to should also enjoy all the benefits of his pleasure. Paul puts it affirmatively in context in 1 Timothy 6:17. "Charge those that are rich in this world, that they not be high-minded, not placing their hope in uncertain riches, but in the living God, *who gives us richly all things to enjoy*" (emphasis added). It is certain that no one can enjoy what is not pleasurable and good. Because God originally designed everything for pleasures, He therefore gives not just few or some of the things He created, but He gives everything to richly enjoy. The character of God is that "Thou lovest righteousness, and hatest wickedness" (Psalm 45:7). The psalmist puts it in a better form in another thorough description: "They shall be abundantly satisfied with the fatness of thy house; and thou shalt make them drink of the river of thy pleasures" (Psalm 36:8).

River of thy pleasures in reference to God. Oh yes. That's the abundance of God's pleasures, because God made everything pleasurably, enjoyable, and full of life and happiness with no limits. God lives in a forever, and all His pleasures are meant to be a forever experienced without any form of obstructions. It's like the ocean, deep and wide and immeasurable. God's pleasures are uncountable and never meant to be seasonal. They are nothing like summer, winter, spring or autumn. The only season of God is one long, unending rivers of pleasures, joy, peace, fellowship, multiplications, supplies, health, wealth, purity, and all that go with these.

It should be noted that the centrality of the message of Christ, the son of God, is anchored on the same theme. All He craved for is to fulfill the will of the heavenly Father, and that is to restore all things to the original plan of God. John 10:10 states, "The thief cometh not, but for to steal, and to kill, and to destroy: I am come that they might have life, and that they might have it more abundantly."

Nothing is worth stealing if it is useless.
Nothing is worth protecting from being killed if it is worthless.
Nothing is worth guarding from being destroyed with the highest power and authority if it is valueless.
Nothing is worth stealing if it is not beneficial.

In another sense, nothing is worth protection from being stolen, being killed and being destroyed with the mightiest power that rules all things in the person of God the Father, God the Son, and God the Holy Spirit if such does not attract their utmost pleasures. God uses all His bests to rescue what was best to Him. God the Father is involved, God the Son is involved, God the Holy Spirit is involved, angels are involved, and He touched the best of humans to work on it from generation to generation until the end of the world.

Health brings pleasures to the body, soul, and spirit of humans, and hence God originally did not create a sick human. When the original plan of God was marred, Jesus, in His earthly ministry, could not help to see sickness but healed them all. In fact, details of His ministry show that in manifold ways are to restore pleasures in all facets of life. The following scriptures attest to this.

The Spirit of the Lord is upon me, because he hath anointed me to preach the gospel to the poor; he hath sent me to heal the brokenhearted, to preach deliverance to the captives, and recovering of sight to the blind, to set at liberty them that are bruised. (Luke 4:18)

How God anointed Jesus of Nazareth with the Holy Spirit and with power, who went about doing good and healing all who were oppressed by the devil, for God was with Him. (Acts 10:38)

Is not this the fast that I have chosen? To loose the bands of wickedness, to undo the heavy burdens, and to let the oppressed go free, and that ye break every yoke? (Isaiah 58:6)

Everything negative in these scriptures is contrary to pleasures, joy, celebration, happiness, praise, and worthiness. The desire of God is to eradicate them wherever they are found because they do not represent the pleasures of a good and loving creator. In fact, left to God, all things coming from Him and through Him should be forever blessed and be blessings to those who have access to them. Hence the Creator of all things never wanted anything to be under a curse. He commands those who believe in Him, "Bless and do not curse" (Romans 12:14). "Out of the same mouth proceedeth blessing and cursing. My brethren, these things ought not so to be. Doth a fountain send forth at the same place sweet water and bitter?" (James 3:10–11). No curse ever brings pleasure, joy, or happiness. No one ever wishes for any form of curse. Curses bring pains, anguish, lamentations, sorrow, regrets, oppression, suppression, and all kinds of unpleasant situations. Blessings are on the contrary. Here is the fundamental expression of a good Creator who designed everything for pleasures: "The blessing of the LORD, it maketh rich, and he addeth no sorrow with it" (Proverbs 10:22).

Abraham's blessings are a showcase of God's delight and what pleasures Him in respect to all his creation.

> Now the Lord had said unto Abram, Get thee out of thy country, and from thy kindred, and from thy father's house, unto a land that I will shew thee:
>
> And I will make of thee a great nation, and I will bless thee, and make thy name great; and thou shalt be a blessing: And I will bless them that bless thee, and curse him that curseth thee: and in thee shall all families of the earth be blessed. (Genesis 12:1–3)

It is in line with the pleasure of God that He made the best choice of land for Abraham and his descendants.

And I have said, I will bring you up out of the affliction of Egypt unto the land of the Canaanites, and the Hittites, and the Amorites, and the Perizites, and the Hivites, and the Jebusites, unto a land flowing with milk and honey. (Exodus 3:17)

And that ye may prolong your days in the land, which the Lord sware unto your fathers to give unto them and to their seed, a land that floweth with milk and honey. For the land, whither thou goest in to possess it, is not as the land of Egypt, from whence ye came out, where thou sowedst thy seed, and wateredst it with thy foot, as a garden of herbs: But the land, whither ye go to possess it, is a land of hills and valleys, and drinketh water of the rain of heaven: A land which the Lord thy God careth for: the eyes of the Lord thy God are always upon it, from the beginning of the year even unto the end of the year. (Deuteronomy 11:9–12).

This certainly presupposes a land of pleasures with the abundance of the goodness of a good God. This generosity and desires of the Creator has been the foundation of things in the original creation. This was meant to be extended to all. This of course will eventually be the ultimate at the consummation of all things in the nearest future. Then it shall be heard throughout eternity: "Thou art worthy, O Lord, to receive glory and honour and power: for thou hast created all things, and for thy pleasure they are and were created" (Revelation 4:11)

Solomon, the wisest king in his generation, has this to say about God's creation with utmost delight and ecstasy: "He hath made *everything beautiful* in his time: also he hath set the world in their heart, so that no man can find out the work that God maketh from the beginning to the end" (Ecclesiastes 3:11; emphasis added). Let's ponder over this statement that every atom of God's creation is beautiful! Anything that's beautiful delights, rejoices, and gives utmost pleasure. Anything opposite of this irritates and is not desirable. This goes to buttress the fact that nothing that emanated from the good Creator was ever meant to not be desirable, delightful, or pleasurable.

The Psalmist praises the works of God thus: "I will praise thee; for I am fearfully and wonderfully made: *marvelous are thy works*; and that my soul knoweth right well" (Psalm 139:14; emphasis added). One can feel the delight and the pleasure of the Psalmist as he extols God with carefully chosen words. *Fearfully* signifies the excellent intricacies and perfection of God's creative prowess. The same description could be ascribed to every single work of God in respect to creation. One can feel the pleasure of the Psalmist as he praises with so much delight the wonders of God's creative prowess. "Wonderfully"! What an epitome of amazement to see the creation of God from every angle and go back to examine it all over again … and yet it's like the more you look, the deeper the appreciation and glorification of the unfathomable creative power and wisdom of God. "Marvelous"! To the psalmist and other beholders, everything that came out as the final product of God's creation attracts so much pleasure and wonders and hence, after all is said and done, achieves the very desires and expectations of the Creator. All the glowing tributes being expressed to praise God for all His wonderful, delightful, and amazing creatures or creations are to God's delight and pleasure. After all, all things were created for His pleasure.

Imagine the episode in Luke 2:8–14.

> And there were in the same country shepherds abiding in the field, keeping watch over their flock by night.
>
> And, lo, the angel of the Lord came upon them, and the glory of the Lord shone round about them: and they were sore afraid. And the angel said unto them, Fear not: for, behold, I bring you good tidings of great joy, which shall be to all people. For unto you is born this day in the city of David a Saviour, which is Christ the Lord. And this shall be a sign unto you; ye shall find the babe wrapped in swaddling clothes, lying in a manger.

And suddenly there was with the angel a multitude
of the heavenly host praising God, and saying, Glory
to God in the highest, and on earth peace, good will
toward men.

Herein are the declarations of the very mind and delight of God
toward His creatures. We see first and foremost the glory of the Lord
overshadowing the shepherds, signifying the presence of God in the
environment. The expression of this was quickly followed by the
interjection of the voice of an angel of God giving humanity a message
from God that there was no need to fear. Where things are good,
awesome, peaceful, pleasurable, and void of death, plagues, anxieties,
pains, terrors, afflictions, hues, and cries, there is no room for any form
of fear. Wherever the presence of the good God is, fear is banished
because everything there must be as God intended. In fact, the presence
of God signifies everything pleasurable to the maximum level with no
iota of evil at all. To buttress the pleasure of God at the announcement
of the angel on the birth of Jesus Christ, the Son of the living God,
who is also referred to as Emmanuel, meaning; "God with us," this
can also mean:

Goodness with us.
Glory with us.
Grace with us.
Greatness with us
Gladness with us.
Guidance with us.
Peace with us.
Protection with us.
Prosperity with us.
Peace with us.
Power with us.
Purity with us.
Pleasurable things with us.
Progress with us.
Perfection with us.

Precious things with us.
Joy with us.
Justice with us.
Jubilee with us.
Live with us.
Health with us.

Blessings with us, holiness with us, delightful things with us, every good and perfect gifts with us, life in abundance with us. No pain, no sorrow, no sickness no anguish, no lack, no limitations. All things with us. In summary, everything that delights God with the fullness of His characteristics with us!

If there is any doubt in respect to the aforementioned attractive and somewhat fantastic notions, hear what came out from the mouth of the angel, who actually was voicing out the message from the Creator: "Fear not: for, behold, I bring you good tidings of great joy, which shall be to all people." I imagine that everything stood still at this moment to hear what the message from God was all about. It was nothing else short of what has been from the beginning of beginnings as to the reason for creation. It was a message to show the mind and desire of a good Creator toward His creatures. It was the very pleasure of God that sort of reverberated throughout the heavens and the earth by the mouth of the angel. The angel says, "I bring you." Wait a minute—bringing from whom to whom? Of course, no angel had personal messages by itself to anyone. They are the messengers of their Creator. The glorious message was from the almighty Creator to his creatures. The message? Good tidings! What a message!

Imagine the delight in the heart of God so eager to send the message of good things! Imagine the delight of the privileged angel that was assigned to make the announcement! Imagine the delight in the hearts of the shepherds that received the good news. The shepherds were, in a sense, representatives of the entire creation. What else can be more delightful than to hear good news? What else can be so more pleasurable than to hear good news? Imagine for a moment a world full of good news twenty-four hours, nonstop! Can there be weeping, mourning, crying, cursing, or fighting? As if that was not enough, the angel went further, saying that the news was not just a good one but of "great joy." The joy originated from the heart of the Creator, because out of the abundance of His pleasure, He gives to his creatures. Therefore the delight and pleasure of God is great joy. Everything that God ever had in mind for His creatures is a maximum level of joy. It is His pleasure that all things under His domain should have this experience and give Him praises and adoration in return. The angel capped the message by saying that the good news of great joy was not only for the immediate recipients but "Which shall be to all people."

Immediately after the angel's announcement, it was as if the windows of heaven were let loose because innumerable eagerly waiting angels flew down in jubilation with praises to God for fulfilling His utmost pleasure, the purpose for which all things were designed. "And suddenly there was with the angel a multitude of the heavenly host praising God, and saying, Glory to God in the highest, and on earth peace, good will toward men." (Luke 2:13-14).What a powerful and wholesome message from these angels! Can anyone imagine how the pleasurable, delightful, jubilant, awesome, joyful, heavenly, never-heard-of, sweetest voices of praises from uncountable holy, powerful, stainless, sinless angels would have sounded? Selah! It must have been a moment when heaven kissed the earth in a kind of joyful honeymoon. The almighty Creator Himself must have been highly elated to watch this happen and put His signature on all that was happening at this point in time.

What a moment that was!

> A moment of joy for which creation was designed.
> A moment of upliftment for which creation was designed.
> A moment of God's will being done on earth as it was in heaven.
> A moment of comfort to all, for which creation was designed.
> A moment when heaven and earth shared sweet fellowship, for which creation was designed.
> A moment of glory, for which creation was designed.
> A moment when God's heart of love yearned for His creature, for which creation was designed.

A moment when God proved His love and goodwill
toward all, for which creation was designed.
A moment when nothing was too precious to spend for
the restoration, for which creation was designed.

What else can bring glory to God in the highest but things that
are good, things that are lovely, things that are joyful, and things that
are pleasurable? The multitudes of angels added two more powerful
messages from the Creator. These two additional messages were to
buttress the fact that was expressed in Jeremiah 29:11, "For I know
the thoughts that I think toward you, saith the LORD, thoughts of
peace, and not of evil, to give you an expected end." The angels
added, "and on earth peace, good will toward men." What could be
more pleasurable than to have peace in all endeavors? Peace with God,
peace within self, peace among all creatures visible and invisible, and
everything good coming from the almighty Creator not just to some
but to all and sundry.

Isn't that the very purpose of creation and what all things were
originally designed for? Isn't this the very pleasure of God for creating
all things? Does any evil, any calamity, any destruction, any pain, any
disaster, any sorrow, any ill luck or bad luck, any disease or malady
give a good God any pleasure? The answer is obvious: no. In fact, the
job description of Jesus Christ, the Son of God, is to "Destroy the
works of the Devil" (1 John 3:8). "For this purpose the Son of God,
was manifested, that he might destroy the works of the devil." Every
work of the devil is never the delight of God, and creatures were never
originally designed for such. In fact, the Bible says in Acts 10:38, "How
God anointed Jesus of Nazareth with the Holy Ghost and with power:
who went about doing good, and healing all that were oppressed of
the devil; for God was with him." God's pleasures are directly related
to the deeds and works of Christ. He never did anything that was the
displeasure of God the Father. He came to carry out the very pleasure
of the Father. He confirmed this also by saying in John 10:10, "The
thief cometh not, but for to steal, and to kill, and to destroy: I am come
that they might have life, and that they might have it more abundantly."
Abundance of what?

Abundance of things that are good.

Abundance of things that are lovely.

Abundance of things that are pleasurable.

Abundance of things that are wonderful.

Abundance of things that are praiseworthy

Abundance of things that are of good report.

Abundance of things for dancing instead of mourning.

Abundance of health instead of sicknesses and afflictions.

Abundance of freedom instead of bondage.

Abundance of life instead of death.

Abundance of gladness instead of sorrow.

Abundance of all things instead of lack.

Abundance of peace instead of confusion and conflict.

Abundance of rest instead of wars and rumors of wars.

The devil does the exact opposite of what the Creator does. In order words, anything that does not bring joy, love, abundance of life, jubilation, glory to the Creator, happiness, peace, or harmony is the very work of the devil. Put it another way, the devil's assignment is to undo the various things that give pleasure to God in respect to the handiwork of God. Because the devil cannot directly cause affliction, steal, kill, or destroy God, he does it indirectly against Him by causing displeasure directly to His creatures. This in turn provokes God to take actions against the devil so He can regain what directly brings Him pleasure, as it was in the beginning.

Paul admonishes all believers to have the mind of Christ and concludes in Philippians 4:8, "Finally, brethren, whatsoever things are true, whatsoever things are honest, whatsoever things are just, whatsoever things are pure, whatsoever things are lovely, whatsoever things are of good report; if there be any virtue, and if there be any praise, think on these things."

"Whatsoever things are true" means things that are definitely opposed to lies. Better still, originals are different from counterfeits. The very true picture of God's intention concerning all his creation was meant to remain in their original and true state of constant and everlasting delight to the Creator. Can you imagine if everything God created had remained in its true state, original state?

"Whatsoever things are honest." The very root of Satanic and Adamic woes stemmed out of dishonesty to the Creator, thereby polluting all the pleasures for which creation was designed.

"Whatsoever things are pure" definitely must be delightful. This originated from the Creator. The purest form of anything is undefiled, uncorrupted, and unpolluted but constantly in the very original, excellent state. Imagine for a moment that Lucifer (now Satan) remained pure and that Adam and Eve remained pure. The story of the entire creation would have been completely delightful.

"Whatsoever things are lovely" definitely must be pleasurable and rejoicing to have the experience of only lovely things:

> Lovely men.
> Lovely women.
> Lovely children.
> Lovely relationships.
> Lovely environment.
> Lovely geo-political systems.
> Lovely desires.
> Lovely aspirations.
> Lovely endeavors.
> Lovely partnerships.
> Lovely cooperation.

Were these not also the very manifestations of God's desires?

"Whatsoever things are just." Imagine that all creatures enjoy the same level of justice at any given time and at all levels.

> Just measure of supplies to all.
> Just measure of peace to all.
> Just measure of joy to all.
> Just measure of love to all.
> Just measure of adequate provisions to all.
> Just measure of protection to all.

Just measure of status to all.
Just measure of power to all.
Just measure of wellbeing to all.

"Whatsoever things are of good report." Who in his or her right mind hates good news? Think about a world of only good news—good reports about all things at all times.

Apostle Paul added virtue—that is to say, anything virtuous toward all, through all, and for all. What an amazing world that is!

To crown it all, Apostle Paul, being in the fullness of the Spirit and certainly having the mind of the Creator, added, "If there be any praise"—anything, anywhere, and at any point in time that is praiseworthy, anything that invokes praises delights God the almighty Creator. The Bible says in Psalm 50:23, "Whoso offereth praise glorifieth me: and to him that ordereth his conversation aright will I shew the salvation of God."

Gloom and praises don't go together.
Lamentations and praises don't go together.
Death and praises don't go together.
Mourning and praises don't go together.
Afflictions and praises don't go together.
Bondage and praises don't go together.
Sighing and praises don't go together.
Defeat and praises don't go together.
Perplexities and praises don't go together.
Pains and praises don't go together.
Sorrow and praises don't go together.
Shame and praises don't go together.

In order words, God's delight and pleasures are on things that bring praise to Him as a Creator. In fact, Apostle Paul says these are the things that believers in God the Creator should think about. In order words, those who believe in God should think like the Creator in whom they believe. They are to have the thought of God. These are the things that pleasure the Creator, and the whole creature was designed for this very purpose.

The only one who ever represented the Creator perfectly on earth was Jesus Christ, the only begotten Son of God. The summary of all that He came to reveal of God the father is as follows.

1. "For God so loved the world that he gave his only begotten Son, that whosoever believeth in him should not perish, but have everlasting life" (John 3:16). A God of love gives all that is good and pleasurable to those He so loves. He gives what will make them happy, delightful, and joyful. He gives nothing evil at all. He cannot give what is good in isolation. It has to affect the environment of the man and the world around him. Not only does God give for a moment of time but perpetually, because he has all the resources to make this a reality. (The everlasting aspect will be dealt with later in this book). Hence the original purpose of God and His pleasures is to satisfy all with good pleasures.

2. "The thief cometh not, but for to steal, and to kill, and to destroy: I am come that they might have life, and that they might have it more abundantly" (John 10:10). Jesus, as the representative of the heavenly Father, reveals in this text that all that has been the original delight and pleasures of God and His creatures had been stolen. Hence all the woes and every unpleasant thing are the order of the day. He now came to restore the lost pleasures of God to all creatures. Real life and living in the original sense was full, joyful, hazard free, danger free, death free, molestation free, sickness and affliction free, fear free—there was absolute freedom as God intended. "Abundant life" as God intended was nothing short of being pleasurable, delightful, joyful, sorrow free, and sin free. Whatever was packed together by God in the original creation was the ultimate plan and purpose of God for all His creatures, visible or invisible, including humans and whatever was in their domain.

3. "How God anointed Jesus of Nazareth with the Holy Ghost and with power: who went about doing good, and healing all

that were oppressed of the devil; for God was with him" (Acts 10:38). To show in a practical sense the very pleasure of God to all creatures, Jesus's major preoccupation on earth was doing good and granting freedom to all who were under any form of oppression or bondage. What great joy it was in the hearts of the people and in the communities of those that God's pleasures were manifested! What great delight and the desire to love to be around Jesus was the case in His earthly ministry. Multitudes chased Him around when they experienced the goodness of God toward them as they were set free by the power of God. In fact, their quest was "give us ever more."

4. "And they were astonished beyond measure, saying, 'He has done all things well'" (Mark 7:37).Can you imagine the joy, the pleasure, the delight, the radiance on the faces of the people who made this statement about Jesus Christ? They were thankful, grateful, glorifying and praising God because the very desire and pleasure of God was demonstrated in their lives. "All things well" is such a significant statement to crown the very purpose of God's creation. It's like echoing what God Himself said in the beginning of creation: "and God saw that all was very good." The master plan and purpose of God for which He set out to bring about creation was to make all things well. And indeed He did make all things well. That was the very design of the almighty Creator.

5. Jesus Christ spoke to His heavenly Father:

> And now I am no more in the world, but these are in the world, and I come to thee. Holy Father, keep through thine own name those whom thou hast given me that they may be one, as we are.
>
> While I was with them in the world, I kept them in thy name: those that thou gavest me I have kept, and none of them is lost, but the son of perdition; that the scripture might be fulfilled.

And now come I to thee; and these things I speak in the world, that they might have my joy fulfilled in themselves. (John 17:11-13).

I pray not that thou shouldest take them out of the world, but that thou shouldest keep them from the evil. (John 17:15).

Father, I will that they also, whom thou hast given me, be with me where I am; that they may behold my glory, which thou hast given me: for thou lovedst me before the foundation of the world. (John 17:24)

Two major things stand out in the prayers and request of Jesus Christ to His heavenly Father.

1. That all that belongs to God be preserved from every form of evil. That is to say, things that do not pleasure God or things that do not bring glory to God. In other words, every form of evil that may be found in creation was not meant to be there at any point in time. They all negate the plan, purpose, and desires of the Creator. They do not represent the pleasure of God at any point in time, wherever and whenever they are found.
2. That all who belong to God should see, enjoy, and partake in the glory of God for all eternity. By this, the very desire for creation in all its ramifications is consummated. In order words, the very pleasures of God. Jesus was advocating, just as the heavenly Father, the full restoration of the lost glory.

Two

THE CREATURES AND THEIR INDIVIDUAL PLEASURES

The Light

"In the beginning God created the heaven and the earth," according to Genesis 1:1. The Bible is the most reliable source of information about the beginning of several things. Let's journey back to the Garden of Eden, where the record of animate and inanimate objects was made known.

The number one delightful thing that was vividly manifest in the garden was the glory of a supernatural brightness. "And God said let there be light, and there was light. And God saw the light." Seeing the wonderful color of the light that shone on the garden was such a glorious delight and unspeakable pleasure even to the Creator, such that it is written that when He saw it, it was "wonderful" and "marvelous," rejoicing the heart of God that He had brought into being what pleasured His heart, and certainly He will bring the same to everything that light will shine upon. Actually, the light was to be a projection of what was inherent in the Creator.

> This then is the message which we have heard of him, and declare unto you, that God is light, and in him is no darkness at all. (1 John 1:5)

God is light. Therefore everything around Him and about Him shines bright and beautifully to the delight of whoever and whatever is around Him. The Bible says "it was good." God is the source of anything and everything that is good. Anything good is always delightful, pleasurable, desirable, lovely, heartwarming, and satisfying. The glow of light beautified whatever else was in the garden. The light beamed on everything in the garden to show forth their beauties and locations for the inhabitants not only to appreciate but to enjoy.

Consider the pleasures derived from light.

1. Visibility of uncountable things far and wide in a moment of time.
2. Establishing attractions to what choices of pleasures to delight the hearts.
3. Bringing things of delight so close by before actually touching them.
4. Putting all the senses to desire and eventually actualizing the desires.
5. Harmonizing and deepening imaginative power for greater creativity in what's on sight.
6. Showing individual aspects of all that is being exposed through the light for greater use by creating more out of little for greater delights.
7. Inspiring the most powerful of the senses, the sense of faith.
8. Making relevance of all things under its rays.
9. Motivating ability to explore.
10. Stimulation of greater and deeper potentials.
11. Creating delightful and desirable ambitions.

Light brings about ultimate pleasures on everything that God created. It showcased all things both great and small. There is no way of acknowledging the goodness and the beauty of all the creatures of God without the light. Everything God created is measured and defined by the amount of light beamed on them.

The Garden of Eden and all within and without it could only be appreciated and fully enjoyed by the presence of the light that revealed what was what, and where was what.

By the light, the pleasure of God was expressed after seeing all that He created as being good and very good.

It was because the light shone on the features of man that inspired the delightful expression of being "fearfully and wonderfully made." It was the light that beamed on the soil that made God to see the awesome usefulness of it and out of it molded a being which He eventually breathed upon to become a living soul. Imagine how it pleasured God to make humans not like any other creature but in His own image. How delightful it is for an artist to put all His best into a masterpiece and at the end exclaim, "This is very good." Is it not out of pleasure? Man himself was designed for God's pleasure. It is said that man was created out of love and for fellowship. You can only fellowship with what you love and have pleasure in.

The very reason why God wants man only for Himself is fellowship of love, and hence He is jealous over man. Exodus 34:14 (KJV) says, "For thou shalt worship no other god: for the Lord, whose name is Jealous, is a jealous God." "And thou shalt love the LORD thy God with all thine heart, and with all thy soul, and with all thy might" (Deuteronomy 6:5). The significance of this is ultimate pleasure. By extension, therefore, every other thing that humans may be engaged in or use or touch is to pleasure the Creator. For humans to continuously be delightful to God and enjoy all the resources of the Creator, they must by all means never transgress to do anything that will displease God. Everything was designed to be in harmony with this objective in mind.

Adam, by the light, was able to see everything in the Garden of Eden, and he was able to differentiate between this and that. When the animals were brought to him, he named them with delight and great pleasure, having seen their features. Here comes the giraffe with the spectacular long neck. What a delight and pleasure for Adam to see that for the first time! (Even today, on a visit to a zoo, especially with little children, see how excited they are to see all manner of animals and birds.) Remember that all things were in a perfect state at the beginning. Adam had the mind of God, and hence all that pleasured God pleasured him too.

God never created anything He had no pleasure in, no matter the shape, color, or stature. If anything came from Him, you can be sure that it was designed for His pleasure. And He put His best in all of them so they might have everything to fulfill His ultimate purpose.

The Bibles says God has given us "all things to richly to enjoy" (1 Timothy 6:17). This presupposes that God created everything for the pleasure of whatever is in the habitat.

The Waters

> And God said, let the waters under the heaven be gathered together unto one place, and let the dry land appear: and it was so.
>
> And God called the dry land Earth; and the gathering together of the waters called he Seas: and God saw that it was good. (Genesis 1:9–10)

Think about the sheer delight of waters suddenly flowing with musical rhythm for the very first time. Oh, the very beautiful outlook of water must have been something gorgeous. Not to talk of the vast expanse of the waters that covered a massive area they were situated. Something more fascinating about this new "liquid stuff" was the pleasurable feeling one could derive from it by simply touching it. How does a man seeing water for the first time react? Wonderful! You desire to hold it tight and not let go. Alas! It slips through your fingers, and all of a sudden the water becomes your playmate. As it falls back to its source, you chase after it to capture, and you fall into the pool of water, and it floats you here and there. Remember that everything was made for pleasure originally, not to kill, drown, or cause any harm. All things were meant to function to show forth the Creator's glory. As 1 Timothy 6:17 states, "Charge them that are rich in this world, that they be not high minded, nor trust in uncertain riches, but in the *living God, who giveth us richly all things to enjoy*" (emphasis added).

You thought you had a good time when the water was touched, but now you are swimming in it, and oh, what a greater delight of feelings that soothe your body and made you desire to stay in it forever. The temperature of the water was just perfect. And what perfect sight was it when the light shone on the water. These helped to make the day a memorable day, a day of great discovery. All of a sudden, you had an intuition of an urge to drink because the Creator wants you to richly enjoy this stuff to His delight and praises. Suddenly you tasted, and your throat wasted no time to pull in the water. Whoa! It was good for drinking too.

So much fun in the sea of delight. The joyful experience of a fulfilled day was accomplished. How can one ever forget the many delights derived from seeing water for the first time, touching the water, drinking the water, swimming in the water, splashing the water, and listening to the musical waves of the waters? Doubtless all things were created for God's pleasure, and they definitely rejoice the heart of the maker and the beneficiaries.

It is another story to mention the delight of the creatures living in the waters and the vegetation that come alive with lovely leaves and flowers, therefore making merry the hearts of all. What a delight to see surface waters including streams, rivers, lakes, reservoirs, and wetlands.

Everything in the beginning enjoyed the presence of light as well as indispensable water. Genesis 2:5–6 says, "And every plant of the field before it was in the earth, and every herb of the field before it grew: for the Lord God had not caused it to rain upon the earth, and there was not a man to till the ground. But there went up a mist from the earth, and watered the whole face of the ground." What a glorious manifestation when rain poured on the earth from heaven for the first time. Imagine the sight, beginning with the clouds artistically forming different shapes and designs on the sky above. Perhaps suddenly a thick cloud appears, mindful of the fact that there was no fear of anything at the beginning of things. Then some gentle breeze blows the trees, and leaves "clap" their hands to welcome the first ever rain drops. Imagine the insects and animals gathering to have a look as well as to have a feel of its refreshing drops or outpouring. All creatures must have gone to sleep dreaming good dreams of that day, thanking the good Creator for doing a new thing to add more fascinating pleasures to the already satisfactory environment. God also must have been very delighted for satisfying His creatures with good things.

To think of the unprecedented and manifold significance of rain. A man of God itemized it as follows.

1. It is a sign of God's pleasure in all and upon all that He brought or brings the rain upon.
2. It is an act to refresh and make room for fruitfulness and multiplication (Leviticus 26:4). Refreshing brings pleasure. Fruitfulness brings pleasure and satisfaction. Multiplication brings fulfillment.
3. It is also a symbol of divine abundant supplies (Exodus 16:4). Anywhere there is abundance directly from God shows the pleasure of God is in manifestation. Dryness and famine are signs of God's displeasure and punishment.
4. Rain is a principal and of high grade among God's good treasure. That is to say, it is one of the most important things in the treasury of God (Deuteronomy 28:12).
5. It is doubtless a symbol of divine favor (Proverbs 16; 15). God can only favor what pleasures Him and what He highly delights in.
6. Rain is certainly a reward from God to show His goodness toward anything that His mercy is upon.

The waters and their surroundings were not only in a perfect state and beautiful to look upon, but countless species of living beings were made to have the time of their lives in them. Everything in the waters was also abundant and full of life. Even the type of life given to the creatures must have been of great essence because everything came from the Almighty, who is perfect in all His doings. In fact, it was to mean that each derived pleasure in each other to the glory of God, their Creator. It must have been of great pleasure to God that despite countless number of things within and around the waters, things had their own distinctions. Some were big, and some were small. Some were tall, and some were short. The whales were different from the catfish, and the crabs were different from the frogs. They all had a mark of perfection, and they were all glorious in diversity.

The Dry Land

> And God said, let the waters under the heaven be gathered together unto one place, and let the dry land appear: and it was so.
>
> And God called the dry land Earth; and the gathering together of the waters called he Seas: and God saw that it was good. (Genesis 1:9–10)

The very idea of the dry land from the sea is to give us the idea of a God who delights in varieties. Variety in the real sense of the word is a yardstick for pleasures. Despite the fact that the seas or the waters and all within and around were more than enough for ultimate satisfaction, God still released yet another fascinating segment of what could be described as simply desirable: the dry land, or the earth.

The waters were full of visible motions with melodies, and the earth was to manifest stillness and somewhat motionless so as to accommodate and sustain whatever God was to create upon it. The mere sight of this new thing spreading all over the length and breadth for as far as the Creator desired must have been of great delight. If there was any praise being offered to the generous Creator at this point in time, my guess is it was this:

> O give thanks unto the LORD; for he is good: because his mercy endureth for ever. (Psalm 118:1)
>
> Blessed be the LORD, who daily loadeth us with benefits, even the God of our salvation. Selah. (Psalm 68:19)

The Almighty God delights in doing one major thing for everything He has made for His praise and glory. It is to daily load all of them with things that are beneficial to enhance their well-being.

> It is to daily load them with pleasures.
> It is to daily load them with joy.

It is to daily load them with peace.
It is to daily load them with prosperity.
It is to daily load them with love.
It is to daily load them with understanding.
It is to daily load them with wisdom.
It is to daily load them with abundance.
It is to daily load them with provisions.
It is to daily load them with happiness.
It is to daily load them with mercies.
It is to daily load them with power.
It is to daily load them with freshness.
It is to daily load them with resources.
It is to daily load them with knowledge.
It is to daily load them with life in its fullness.
It is to daily load them with necessary supplies.

They can be attested to in the scriptures.

> It is of the Lord's mercies that we are not consumed, because his compassion fail not. They are new every morning: great is thy faithfulness. (Lamentations 3:22–23 KJV)

> But my God shall supply all your need according to his riches in glory by Christ Jesus. (Philippians 4:19)

All these are in line with the very desires and designs of God.

The Grass, the Herbs, the Trees, and the Fruits

True to the nature and the pleasure of the Creator, what followed next was no longer a surprise. The dry land coming from God could not but bring forth something good. Nothing coming from God ever had any iota of evil, displeasure, or damnation.

> And God said, let the earth bring forth grass, the herb yielding seed, and the fruit tree yielding fruit after his kind, whose seed is in itself, upon the earth: and it was so.
>
> And the earth brought forth grass, and herb yielding seed after his kind, and the tree yielding fruit, whose seed was in itself, after his kind: and God saw that it was good. (Genesis 1:11–12)

The appearance of the grass, herbs, and trees of different types, shapes, and sizes filling the entire landscape must have been ecstatic. What a wonder to witness hitherto never seen green grass well groomed and situated at the appropriate locations to beautify the land. How about the trees that must have not been haphazardly placed or planted here and there but were well positioned in perfect order of size and shape? This is in line with the Creator's way of doing things: "Let all things be done decently and in order" (1 Corinthians 14:40). Imagine the beauty of the entire land with such a magnificent orderliness of all the trees and herbs and grass. To cap it all, the "herb yielding seed, and the fruit tree yielding fruit after his kind, whose seed is in itself."

All manner of fruits! Oh, my world, with different kinds of pleasurable tastes in their organic and original form. A visit to orange tree would satisfy and give a different taste of fruit from water that had been hitherto. Let's have a look at some of the fruits, one after another.

Imagine seeing the array of different types of fruits and their shapes and sizes, as well as their leaves and the plants upon which they hang. The tastes were original, the eater with the original sense of taste and right appetite for them. Picking and having a close look at each of the fruits is an amazing experience, let alone having a taste of each of them. Don't they look delightful and pleasurable?

Let's visit the pineapple. You are forced to have a closer look with such admiration as to why a small tree will produce such a big fruit with a unimaginable wonderful design. The fruit itself is embroidered in fascinating, mathematical columns and cells. On top of the fruit are leaves pointing toward heaven as if stretching forth their hands of thanksgiving to their Creator. And now to the taste of this juicy fruit is another wonder to the palate. So refreshing, and nothing short of satisfaction and pleasure. Indeed, God "giveth us all things richly to enjoy" (1 Timothy 6:17 KJV).

But there are still more!

Pawpaw fruit is also beckoning for a taste of pleasure and delight. Whoa! There is no use comparing this with the previous one. The tree is different, taller. The leaves are different too, and now to the very fruit, this time with many on a single tree and of different sizes and shapes! What a Creator with absolute ingenuity and creativity. He meticulously designed each one so much so that even though they are so many types of fruits, one cannot be mistaken for the other. This is to show pleasure in diversities both from the Creator and for the creatures.

One other thing fascinating about these fruits are the means through which they can be reproduced. Some can be reproduced through seeds, and the seeds are different in shape and sizes as well. Some are reproduced by simply replanting the branches of the trees that bear the fruits. This in itself is delightful.

Wonders will never end as one approaches the coconut tree. The shell that covers the fruit is so hard that seeing it for the first time will give you much to ponder over as to how to get into the fruit. The layers of security and the tallness of the tree, coupled with the very shape, is mind-burgling compared with the two fruits earlier described. The mere thought of how to get into the fruit fascinates the eater, thereby having to depend on the wisdom of God in a delightful manner to get an answer. The more you see, the more you want to explore. The more you experience, the more honor and glory and reverence are attributed to the Creator, which is actually His delight.

> Praise ye the Lord. Praise, O ye servants of the Lord, praise the name of the Lord. Blessed be the name of the Lord from this time forth and for evermore.

From the rising of the sun unto the going down of the same the Lord's name is to be praised. The Lord is high above all nations, and his glory above the heavens.

Who is like unto the Lord our God, who dwelleth on high,

Who humbleth himself to behold the things that are in heaven, and in the earth!

He raiseth up the poor out of the dust, and lifteth the needy out of the dunghill;

That he may set him with princes, even with the princes of his people.

He maketh the barren woman to keep house, and to be a joyful mother of children. Praise ye the Lord. (Psalm 113:1- 9 KJV).

Another fruit? Perhaps mango will be attracting attention for a juicy taste of a different kind. How about the pomegranates, apples, plantains, bananas, blackberries, grapes, apricots, blackberries, avocado, blueberries, black currant, breadfruit, cantaloupe, cherries, cherimoya, cranberries, custard apples, date fruits, durian, elderberries, feijoa, figs, grapefruits, guava, gooseberries, honeydew melons—on and on and on. For what purpose could all these fruits have been made available if not for pleasure, for enjoyment, and for ultimate satisfaction, thereby arousing the giving of praises and adoration to the generous Creator? No wonder the people of God are admonished in Deuteronomy 6:10-12 "And it shall be, when the LORD thy God shall have brought thee into the land which he sware unto thy fathers, to Abraham, to Isaac, and to Jacob, to give thee great and goodly cities, which thou buildedst not, And houses full of all good things, which thou filledst not, and wells digged, which thou diggedst not, vineyards and olive trees, which thou plantedst not; when thou shalt have eaten and be full; Then beware lest thou forget the LORD, which brought thee forth out of the land of Egypt, from the house of bondage."

It is said that there are over two thousand types of known fruits. It's unimaginable how wonderful, delightful, and pleasurable an experience it will be having to taste each of them. Have a critical look at the very nature, design, and inward and outward look of these fruits in their natural habitats. The Creator had this array of pleasant fruits, and the variety of tastes had only one primary desire in His mind: for the pleasures and well-being of all His creatures, that He might satisfy them with good things and quench their God-given appetites, good cravings, delight, and enjoyment. This goes to show that God is a God of satisfaction in the realm of good things. Good things, good tastes, varieties, and abundance of all things bring satisfaction, joy, happiness, and gladness at all levels of life to the Creator and the creatures. To cap it all, He allows the fruits to come forth in their seasons so that the expectations of His creatures are never disappointed. Hence the scripture says, "For the Lord God is a sun and shield: the Lord will give grace and glory: no good thing will he withhold from them that walk uprightly" (Psalm 84:11 KJV). God will not withhold anything pleasant, satisfying, delightful, joyful, praiseworthy, or pleasurable from those that belong to Him. Hence, praises go to Him.

> Bless the Lord, O my soul: and all that is within me, bless his holy name.
>
> Bless the Lord, O my soul, and forget not all his benefits:
>
> Who redeemeth thy life from destruction; who crowneth thee with lovingkindness and tender mercies?
>
> Who satisfieth thy mouth with good things; so that thy youth is renewed like the eagle's. (Psalm 103:1–5 KJV)

A good song that could be rendered to the good God while tasting these fruits could be

Oh Lord My God, when I in Awesome Wonder,
Consider all the worlds Thy hands have made;
I see the stars, I hear the rolling thunder,
Thy power throughout the universe displayed.

Then sings my soul, My Savior God, to Thee,
How great Thou art! How great Thou art!

—Carl Boberg, 1885

Some wonderful benefits of these fruits cannot be overlooked. The care and well-being of God's creatures are of great concern to Him.

Fruit is said to be one of the most healthy and natural foods in existence. It's amazing that there are not just hundreds of them but thousands, all of which provide us with strong health benefits. Fruit contains a large number of naturally occurring vitamins, minerals, and plant petrochemicals that help benefit health.

- Potential for weight control
- More energy for exercising
- Reduced risk of cardiovascular diseases
- Reduced risk of developing cancers
- Lower blood pressure
- Potential to lower cholesterol
- Reduced risk of developing type-2 diabetes
- Potential to slow down the aging process

Vegetables

Fruits, fruits, fruits everywhere in their thousands should be abundant enough to enrich the lives of humans. But the Creator's pleasure is never limited, and hence He adds variety of vegetables. Good God!

Vegetables are also in their hundreds for the benefit of all. It is said that there are more than two hundred types of vegetables available. There are in different shapes and colors with manifold delightful, awesome, and fascinating shapes. Pick lettuce and be charmed with the manifold leaves; and unwrap one leaf to get to another, and on and on.

Carrot is standing erect in its yellow corner like an unbendable stick, yet it is easy to bend, break, and munch. How about spinach, potatoes, mustard, and onions?

A closer look at the variety of these vegetables makes you wonder how the Creator can put so much efforts in designing them inwardly and outwardly—the roots and the leaves, their different tastes, and even creative ways of enjoying them.

It is great pleasure to go into the fields of the green ones, yellow ones, purples, blues, and reds and gaze at them with delight even before tasting them.

Simply put, seeing and having access to all these cannot but produce an overwhelming joy of God's pleasure, resulting in gratitude with a shout of, "How great Thou art!"

Vegetables are helpful for the following reasons.

> To fight bloat and keep the digestive system healthy
> To create youthful glow
> To reduce stress
> To protect bones
> To provide complex carbohydrates
> To provide cancer-fighting agents
> To maintain healthy blood pressure
> To reduce blood cholesterol levels and may lower risk
> of heart disease
> To help the body form red blood cells
> To help heal cuts and wounds, and to keep teeth and
> gums healthy.

An old adage is, "Health is wealth." I wish to add that the combination of both health and wealth is reasonably happy, joyful, and peaceful, and life is full of good pleasures as the Creator intended.

WONDERS ABOVE

While still surveying the amazing things below on earth, the Creator shifts His gaze to bring about more fascinating things far above.

> And God said, let there be lights in the firmament of the heaven to divide the day from the night; and let them be for signs, and for seasons, and for days, and years:
>
> And let them be for lights in the firmament of the heaven to give light upon the earth: and it was so. And God made two great lights; the greater light to rule the day, and the lesser light to rule the night: he made the stars also.
>
> And God set them in the firmament of the heaven to give light upon the earth,
>
> And to rule over the day and over the night, and to divide the light from the darkness: and God saw that it was good. (Genesis 1:14–16)

The Creator has a perfect sense of delight in surrounding everything He has created with much beauty. Hence every aspect and the minute details of all His creatures are full of wonders and awe. While still gazing at the marvelous works from beneath, the Creator takes the eyes and gaze of the beholder to what He can see and admire but far away from his touch and taste. The Creator, so to say, attaches or glues some fascinating objects that are glorious in outlook and pleasant to look upon far away in the sky. Genesis1:14 says, "And God said, let there be lights in the firmament of the heaven to divide the day from the night; and let them be for signs, and for seasons, and for days, and years."

They are to beautify the earth with their immaculate lights and also to give a sense of time and seasons so that living will not be too monotonous. God, who has originally designed all things for benefits, delight, pleasures, and good for all, even basks in the monotonous—that is to say, in the repetition of good things, good feelings, and pleasurable activities that glorify Him. At the same time, He also delights in varieties for His pleasure and that of His creatures. Hence the creation of the lights in the firmament for days and nights, the seasons, and the years. Imagine the anticipation of a good night when the day is over, and that of a good day when the day is dawning. Oh, what a pleasant feeling to anticipate new things, new days, new months, and new years and to see the various signs that accompany them. Life was never meant to be boring or static. Simply put, everything was designed to be full of live and for maximum benefit.

The Sun

The sun is said to be at an average distance of about 93 million miles (150 million kilometers) away from Earth. It is so far away that light from the sun, traveling at a speed of 186,000 miles (300,000 kilometers) per second, takes about eight minutes to reach the earth. Apart from giving a bright shining light that illuminates everything under its radar, it is by far the most important source of energy for life on Earth. The energy of this sunlight supports almost all life on Earth by photosynthesis, and it drives Earth's climate and weather.

The fascinating thing about this gigantic object is that the Creator hangs it on whatever. One cannot but be amazed at the radiance of it but the key of control is only with the Creator. One could less agree with the composers of the poems on the sunshine below.

Let the Sunshine In

Let the sunshine in, let the sunshine in;
Open up your hearts and let the sunshine in.

I got a friend in you; you got a friend in me.
Just smile that way each and every day,
fill the world with love and say!

Let the sunshine in, let the sunshine in;
Open up your hearts and let the sunshine in.

—Purcy Flaherty, August 2018

Step into the Sunshine

Step into the sunshine my friend,
let it kiss your face and refine your spirit into a golden bar.

Step into the sunshine my friend,
come out of the shadows of your past,
emerge as a saintly being clothed in angelic white.

...

Step into the sunshine my friend,
wipe the darkness from your eyes
see what miracles the new day brings.

—James Bradley McCallum, March 2013

Some benefits of sunshine are staggering.

1. Sun exposure lowers blood pressure.
2. Sun exposure improves bone health.
3. Sun exposure improves brain function.
4. Sun exposure eases mild depression.
5. Sun exposure improves sleep quality.
6. Sun exposure lessens Alzheimer's symptoms.
7. Sun exposure heals some skin disorders.
8. Sun exposure improves brain function.
9. Sun exposure improves heart health.
10. Sun exposure impacts on depression.
11. Sun exposure boosts immunity.
12. Sun exposure reduces risk of cancer.
13. Sun exposure improves your mood.
14. Sun exposure impacts active life.

In fact, life as humans understand it isn't possible on Earth without the sun, because the water would be frozen.

The sun benefits the Earth by giving the light by which animals see, or the energy they need in order to produce artificial light. The heat makes life on Earth possible, and it provides energy for plants to make food through photosynthesis of sunlight. Some living things exist in dark places on our planet, but almost all life as we know it depends on the sun. Plants also make the oxygen that we breathe.

Only the pleasure of the Creator could have brought this into being for the maximum enjoyment of all beings, coordinated together.

What more is this than a sight of pleasures and the energy it brings to awaken the mood to a delightful and active life? Where there is energy, there are accomplishments. Accomplishments bring about fulfillment, and fulfillment brings about satisfaction, thereby making each day praiseworthy to the Creator.

This is the LORD'S doing; it is marvelous in our eyes.

This is the day which the LORD hath made; we will rejoice and be glad in it.(Psalm 118:23-24)

The Moon

While still pondering and appreciating wonders and the beauty of the sun, lie down to gaze at the firmament and see another object rolling out from only God knows from where, shining and smiling at the same time in the cool of the night. It becomes another product of amazing delight. We thought we've seen them all, and we thought we had more than enough, but the Creator had not finished the project of His delight. Here comes the moon, adorned with the brightness to beautify the night and everything under its radar as well.

After the sun, the moon is the second brightest celestial object visible in the sky. Only about 59 percent of the moon's surface can actually be seen from Earth. Some benefits of the moon will certainly convince us again and again that all things were originally designed for pleasures. It's all about good things to richly enjoy and make all the creatures happy and joyful so they might praise Him, because "the LORD is good to all: and his tender mercies are over all his works" (Psalm 145:9).

1. Relief from insomnia
2. Remarkable concentration abilities
3. Correction of eye problems such as myopia, farsightedness, and the early stages of cataracts (I haven't verified this, but it's a common claim)
4. Development of the third eye and intuitive abilities.
5. Deep relaxation and many of the other benefits that can be received from godly meditation

In the light of the goodness of God, everything created has potential to bring about joy, happiness, and ultimate pleasures, as well the awe and admiration of God. The Psalmist says in Psalm 145:10–13 (KJV),

> All thy works shall praise thee, O Lord; and thy saints shall bless thee.
>
> They shall speak of the glory of thy kingdom, and talk of thy power;
>
> To make known to the sons of men his mighty acts, and the glorious majesty of his kingdom. Thy kingdom is an everlasting kingdom, and thy dominion endureth throughout all generations.

There is an emphasis on all the works of God, without any exception. All the works of GOD are to bring Him praises, adoration, and thanksgiving. If they are meant for anguish, punishment, oppression, burdens, or anything contrary to good use and good purposes, then they will not have any attachment to praises. But all were designed to praise Him.

In fact, the Lord does not withhold, and He never intended to withhold anything He enjoyed or had pleasure in to elude any of His creatures. Hence it is written concerning the Israelites of old.

> All the commandments which I command thee this day shall ye observe to do, that ye may live, and multiply, and go in and possess the land which the Lord sware

unto your fathers. Thy raiment waxed not old upon thee, neither did thy foot swell, these forty years.

For the Lord thy God bringeth thee into a good land, a land of brooks of water, of fountains and depths that spring out of valleys and hills;

A land of wheat, and barley, and vines, and fig trees, and pomegranates; a land of oil olive, and honey;

A land wherein thou shalt eat bread without scarceness, thou shalt not lack any thing in it; a land whose stones are iron, and out of whose hills thou mayest dig brass.

When thou hast eaten and art full, then thou shalt bless the Lord thy God for the good land which he hath given thee.

Lest when thou hast eaten and art full, and hast built goodly houses, and dwelt therein. And when thy herds and thy flocks multiply, and thy silver and thy gold is multiplied, and all that thou hast is multiplied;

But thou shalt remember the Lord thy God: for it is he that giveth thee power to get wealth that he may establish his covenant which he sware unto thy fathers, as it is this day. (Deuteronomy 8:1, 4, 7–13, 18 KJV)

What more could God do than to make the people maximally possess the rivers of His pleasures? Canaan was designed as heaven on earth for them. Imagine if there was no sin, no rebellion, and no disobedience. The very pleasures of God would have forever flown unhindered. It was the picture of the very design of God.

Nothing was designed to be old, to be sickly, to be fruitless, to be cursed, to be in any bad shape, to be lonely, to lack any good thing, to be famished, or to reduce or stagnate. All things were created for God's pleasure that they might have live and have it more abundantly.

The Stars

The sun to rule the day and the moon to rule the night—that should have been more than enough for happy days and delightful nights, as well as times and seasons. But there was still more to come out of the reservoirs of God's pleasures. His creative power, prowess, and propensity will not let go until He let out all His desires for the utmost benefits of all His creatures. He needs more praises, more honors, and more adoration so that everything under His dominion will never seize to wonder who this magnificent Creator really is. Because God is omniscient, whatever He supervises has to be perfect.

Read what Moses said in Deuteronomy 32:1–14.

> Give ear, O ye heavens, and I will speak; and hear, O earth, the words of my mouth.
>
> My doctrine shall drop as the rain, my speech shall distil as the dew, as the small rain upon the tender herb, and as the showers upon the grass:
>
> Because I will publish the name of the LORD: ascribe ye greatness unto our God.
>
> He is the Rock, his work is perfect: for all his ways are judgment: a God of truth and without iniquity, just and right is he.
>
> Do ye thus requite the LORD, O foolish people and unwise? Is not he thy father that hath bought thee? hath he not made thee, and established thee?
>
> Remember the days of old, consider the years of many generations: ask thy father, and he will shew thee; thy elders, and they will tell thee.
>
> When the most High divided to the nations their inheritance, when he separated the sons of Adam, he

set the bounds of the people according to the number of the children of Israel.

For the LORD'S portion is his people; Jacob is the lot of his inheritance.

He found him in a desert land, and in the waste howling wilderness; he led him about, he instructed him, he kept him as the apple of his eye.

As an eagle stirreth up her nest, fluttereth over her young, spreadeth abroad her wings, taketh them, beareth them on her wings:

So the LORD alone did lead him, and there was no strange god with him.

He made him ride on the high places of the earth, that he might eat the increase of the fields; and he made him to suck honey out of the rock, and oil out of the flinty rock;

Butter of kine, and milk of sheep, with fat of lambs, and rams of the breed of Bashan, and goats, with the fat of kidneys of wheat; and thou didst drink the pure blood of the grape.

What a magnificent song in honor of the wonderful Creator. History classified Moses as one of the greatest men who ever knew God as Creator. In fact, he was the man God used to reveal to the entire world the beginning of all things created by God in the book of Genesis. Moses wrote without mincing words that the work of God is perfect, both great and small, visible or invisible. Anything perfect definitely attracts first-class admiration, delight, and fascination, and in the end that pleases the admirers or the possessors.

Solomon, who was the wisest king of his generation, buttressed the same point in Ecclesiastes 3:9–14 (NKJV).

What profit has the worker from that in which he labors? I have seen the God-given task with which the sons of men are to be occupied. He has made everything beautiful in its time. Also He has put eternity in their hearts, except that no one can find out the work that God does from beginning to end.

I know that nothing is better for them than to rejoice, and to do good in their lives, and also that every man should eat and drink and enjoy the good of all his labor—it is the gift of God.

I know that whatever God does,
it shall be forever.
Nothing can be added to it,
And nothing taken from it.
God does it, that men should fear before Him.

Solomon emphasizes the fact that it is the gift of God to richly enjoy whatsoever He has given to humankind. He also pointed out that whatsoever God does, nothing can be added to it, and nothing can be taken from it. This is to say that cut from any angle, all that comes from God will never need to be perfected because nothing is ever going to be better than whatever the Creator has made. Therefore all that is left is to stand in awe of Him and bask in enjoying His goodness. What, then, could be more pleasurable than to have the best, know the best, experience the best, see the best, feel the best, and touch the best? It was certainly God's original design.

And now to show more of His creative power and delight, God decided to decorate the firmament with more wonders by way of innumerable stars. It is estimated that there are over one hundred billion stars! This is mind-boggling!

While gazing up to the sky, one cannot but join the poet in wondering,

Twinkle, twinkle, little star,
How I wonder what you are!
Up above the world so high,
like a diamond in the sky.

When the blazing sun is gone,
when he nothing shines upon,
Then you show your little light,
Twinkle, twinkle, all the night.
—Jane Taylor (1783–1824)

Come to think of it, even the smallest stars are pretty big compared to the Earth. For instance, it is said that stars like Trappist-1 or Proxima Centauri are ten times the size, or diameter, of Earth. The sun is nearly one hundred times larger. And the largest stars are 150,000 times the diameter of Earth.

Isn't it beyond fascinating to have a glimpse of the array of these stars far away from the earth beneath? What about having the opportunity to go near each of them and touch, feel, and move around for years and years unending? The expression and feelings will be beyond description. All the splendor, all the brightness, all the spectacular arrangements, all the levels of height, length, and breadth of them are doubtlessly breathtaking, yet surpassing all these are great pleasures in taking a tour among the billions of shining stars.

INSIDE THE WATERS AND CREATURES IN THE FIRMAMENT

There is something unique about God, the master Creator: the supreme attention to details, quality of the highest order, and quantity. Much as He delights in varieties, at the same time He enjoys all His creatures being so uniquely formed, yet He wants them in abundance. He wants all things to be more than enough for everyone to richly enjoy. It is the nature of a peace lover to delight in making more than enough for everyone, so much so that there is no room for any form of struggle or strife. No wonder goodness was inscribed on everything that God originally made. The signature of God never came upon anything He ever considered good enough in His sight or good enough for the benefits of the users. Goodness in itself is a representation of pleasures.

Therefore to expand and extend the measures of His goodness, God never stopped in His fabulous works of creation until He finds room for all He desired. Therefore He was not satisfied with a hollow expanse of rivers and oceans without having to fill them up with moving creatures great and small. And the skies were too timid for Him not to find some moving objects to furnish them with. God of wonders!

Genesis 1:20–21 says, "And God said, Let the waters bring forth abundantly the moving creature that hath life, and fowl that may fly above the earth in the open firmament of heaven. And God created great whales, and every living creature that moveth, which the waters brought forth abundantly, after their kind, and every winged fowl after his kind: and God saw that it was good."

There is so much to see already, so much to taste already, so much to eat and drink. Yet the more you see, the more there is to see. The more you taste, the more there is to taste. The more wonders you find, the more there is to discover. There is an abundance of moving creatures in the firmament!

These are also of diverse in outlook. Some are tiny and some are big, yet they all fly at various levels. Some are multicolored, and some just black, blue, yellow, green, or white. What in the heavens suspends these fascinating objects in the air? They play, they meander on the air. They fly low and suddenly take off to an oblivion far out of sight. Some fly alone, and some move in groups. They do it with ease and great pleasure, as was divinely ordained.

Wait a minute—there is still more about them. They sing. What a wonder of wonders! And for that matter, they have different tunes and tones. All that could be said of these fascinating objects in respect to the awesome creator is,

> The heavens declare the glory of God; and the firmament sheweth his handywork.

Day unto day uttereth speech, and night unto night sheweth knowledge.

There is no speech nor language, where their voice is not heard.

Their line is gone out through all the earth, and their words to the end of the world. In them hath he set a tabernacle for the sun,

Which is as a bridegroom coming out of his chamber, and rejoiceth as a strong man to run a race.

His going forth is from the end of the heaven, and his circuit unto the ends of it: and there is nothing hid from the heat thereof. (Psalm 19:1-6 KJV)

The beauty of these flying objects is also in the fact that they are of various species: the birds, the insects, and the bats.

The Birds

It is said that there are over ten thousand living species of birds. Imagine seeing the array of these birds displaying their agility in flight at the same time and singing various melodies in the ears of those that had the original sensibility to decode the meanings. What a fellowship, what a divine joy that will be. Talk of delight, talk of admiration. Talk of uninterrupted and uncorrupted pleasure! Some of these birds were also designed not only to fly; some species are of aquatic environments, especially seabirds and some water birds, and hence they display swimming prowess too.

It's amazing to watch the ways in which they communicate, relate, lay eggs, build their nests, incubate eggs, hatch the eggs, and nurture the chicks until they are able to fly.

Here is another fact that beats one's imagination in respect to some of these fragile but powerful creatures in great exploits: Many bird species are said to migrate to faraway places across the globe to take advantage of seasonal temperatures. Migration is very demanding energetically, particularly to birds because of the need to cross deserts and oceans without drinking or feeding along the way. According to Wikipedia article on birds, Land birds, for instance, are said to have a flight range of over two thousand kilometers. Shorebirds can fly up to four thousand kilometers. The bar-tailed godwit is said to be capable of non-stop flights of up to ten thousand kilometers. Seabirds also undertake long migrations, the longest annual migration being those of sooty shearwaters, whose an annual round trip could be up to an amazing over sixty kilometers

Wouldn't it be wonderful to journey with each of these species from territory to territory? It sure will be the enjoyable ride of a lifetime. The bliss of sightseeing all the landscape below from their lofty heights, all things both great and small, all things on the hills and mountains, all things in the valleys and the seas, all things in motion and static … All for pleasure and for free.

Think about the shared joy of watching flamingos; the stunningly beautiful golden, silver, and ring-necked pheasants; crane birds; the gorgeous, multicolor peacocks; mandarin ducks, and Victoria crowned pigeons, to mention but a few.

Only a God of pleasures can meticulously and awesomely have a thought to design each of these birds with unique features in outlook, and they are perfectly beautiful to behold. He used all His might, all His interests, all His wisdom, knowledge, and understanding unique to Him alone to design all of them. So masterfully did He create them that no one can ever dispute or even wish to add or take away from the perfection of any of them. They all meet the maximum pleasure and glory of His good thoughts toward them. Surely He has made all things beautiful in His time.

This is to confirm that whatever God makes and whenever He makes or made them, they meet the standard of excellence and beauty. They are praiseworthy and bring glory to Him. The summary, therefore, is that they all address the same subject matter, making them pleasurable.

The Insects

Insects are said to be the most diverse group of animals, and there are more than a million known species representing more than half of all known living organisms. Their shapes, colors, and makeup are truly amazing.

It is a great delight, for instance, watching some of them undergo a four-stage metamorphosis: egg, larva, pupa, and adult. In each stage of metamorphosis, the animal looks different than at the other stages. Imagine the emergence of a beautiful, multicolored butterfly out of a tiny egg. Watching each stage of development with rapt attention and seeing the end product of God's design is glorious! Can anyone hold back adoration, fascination, delight, and a sense of awe about these wonders if he had all the time to observe all the stages of development and activities of all the millions of these insects in their natural habitats?

> And after these things I heard a great voice of much people in heaven, saying, Alleluia; Salvation, and glory, and honor, and power, unto the Lord our God. (Revelation 19:1 KJV)

> And they sing the song of Moses the servant of God, and the song of the Lamb, saying, great and marvelous are thy works, Lord God Almighty. (Revelation 15:3)

The conclusion of the whole matter is this: great and marvelous are the works of God without any exception. Anything that is great and at the same time marvelous calls for great delight, great admiration, great applause, great fascination and the end point is pleasurable in the good sense of the word. This was exactly the divine expectations of the Creator.

It's staggering to note that some of the insects can combine flight with swimming and walking. They also produce wonderful things for the good of other creatures. Think about the bees and the sweet honey. How about the butterflies pollinating our flowers? The list goes on and on. To cap it all, take a closer look at their wings, eyes, colors, and legs which are in their own rights amazing!

Abundance in the Waters

Suffice it to say at this juncture that all the aforementioned creatures of God, though not fully defined or described as much as they are worth, talk less of being close to how deep the Creator will have us see in them. Yet these are the tip of the iceberg with respect to other designs and creatures of God.

Let's see some of the abundance in the waters. Genesis 1:20–21 states, "And God said, Let the waters bring forth abundantly the moving creature that hath life, and fowl that may fly above the earth in the open firmament of heaven. And God created great whales, and every living creature that moveth, which the waters brought forth abundantly, after their kind, and every winged fowl after his kind: and God saw that it was good."

One emphasis must always be burned in one's mind: God's stamp of approval on everything He created as being good. This is doubtless a reflection of His excitement, joy, gladness, satisfaction, and delight, and to show how pleased He has been with all his creatures. Everything created is good for its purposes—good to behold, good for every reason, good in appearance, worth feeling good about, good to touch, good for fellowship, good to have, good to reproduce, good to multiply, good to appreciate. Nothing less could be said of every creation of God than what He said of them. Why? Because they all have been made to meet the highest standard, as well as specifications of His good pleasure. Hence they were therefore created to be at their very best.

And so, here come the numerous moving, living creatures in the waters. Water, all alone by itself, is delightful. But now the addition of millions of moving creatures to swim in the massive rivers of God's delight is something else entirely. Though the moving creatures are in their millions as well as diverse in shape and sizes, there is more than enough room for both great and small, enough sustenance for both great and small, enough resources for both great and small, enough current for both great and small.

It's not surprising to point out that there are over two hundred thousand known species of living creatures in the ocean—and as many as two million more that remain a total mystery. This is doubtless a whopping number hard to digest. It's beyond comprehension to just walk to the seaside and have all of them line up at the bays, stretching an expanse of several miles in distance. What if it was possible for someone to have a closer look at all the features of each of them, have a feel, a touch, and a conversation? How about watching all the various activities of each of these millions uninterrupted by time, fatigue, or anything else? When all is said and done, if such an entity is interviewed as to what were his experiences at the end of many years of his expenditure, how many books will be written in praises, adoration, and gratitude about an awesome God the Creator?

But aside from this, the individual will certainly come to the same conclusion that all things were created for His pleasure, not only for the Creator but certainly for the pleasure of everyone.

Granted that all these creatures should be allowed to display their swimming skills (similar to a sporting event), one by one. Think about the memorable delight of the dolphin mesmerizing in the ocean and then have a look at the cat fish doing its own according to its ability. Then all of a sudden, the mighty whale surfaces, and the water sort of roars, and the jellyfish finds its level. The crabs say, "We are here too," while the sea snakes meander across.

Let's pulse awhile from the swimming display of millions of these sea creatures to point out that it's been proved that there are more than eighteen thousand known species of fish alone. It will be an amazing sight to see each and every one of them!

> Immortal, invisible, God only wise,
> In light inaccessible hid from our eyes,
> Most blessed, most glorious, the Ancient of Days,
> Almighty, victorious, thy great Name we praise.

To all life thou givest—to both great and small;
In all life thou livest, the true life of all;
We blossom and flourish as leaves on the tree,
And wither and perish—but nought changeth thee.
—Walter Chalmers Smith (1867)

These sea creatures are also incredibly colorful, amazingly beautiful. That's something common in all of God's creatures: colorful, beautiful, elegant, fascinating, delightful, awe-inspiring, praiseworthy, and culminating in pleasures when all aspects are critically examined. How about a look at the clownfish, or the blue sea slug, lizardfish, sea turtle, sharks, dolphins, flying fishes, and the elephant seal? How about the manatees, or the tiny plankton and other sea inhibiters countless in number? There are still room enough for the big walrus, the deep sea giant isopod, and countless others.

Probing and meticulously researching into all these millions of sea creatures in full detail with respect to their sizes, shapes, colors, how they move and live on a daily basis, how they play and reproduce, how they sleep, and how they make use of all the parts of their bodies is nothing short of incredible in the real sense of the word.

A close look at majestic features of the sharks is magnificent. It's said that there are over one thousand species of them. They range in size from the small to the *Rhincodon typus*, or whale shark, the largest fish in the world, which reaches approximately twelve meters (forty feet) in length. One will be fascinated by the appearance of the tiger shark, but here come the blue shark, great white shark, mako shark, thresher shark, and hammerhead shark, all majestically dominating their spheres of jurisdiction with such pomp and pageantry!

It should be noted what was God's unequivocal pronouncement on all of them: "and God blessed them." Every one of these creatures both great and small originally received nothing but the blessings of the Creator. Imagine a wealthy man blessing everything around him with all affordable riches. The questions, then, are, How rich is God the Creator? What kind of blessings did He bestow on all His creatures? For how long were the blessings supposed to last?

God, who never possessed any evil by any means, bestowed His pleasure of blessings upon them all. Blessing portends favor, protection, having all good means, manifold benefits without harms, all-around enjoyment without stress, goodness and mercies, soundness in every area, love, living well, and being in a state of satisfaction. If this was the case, all these creatures were designed to for ever enjoy all these benefits. It was meant to make them happy, and provisions were to be supplied perpetually, at all times and in all seasons from their Maker.

The Creator, being rich in all things and being mindful of them at all times even before He ever thought of bringing them into being, had made all provisions available for them to thrive. Subsequent to creating anything at all, He made sure resources were available for their sustenance. Hence before He ever created the moving objects on the air, the conditions were already in place for flight to be conducive, and space was made ready with the air to aid flying. By the same token, the sea and ocean were already in place in abundance before the sea creatures were created to inhabit them. Hence the natural habitat of all God's creatures are perfectly suitable for them to live and live abundantly to the point of pleasures of diverse magnitudes, to the end they can appreciate and give glory to the Creator. And on the other end, the Creator might rejoice over his handiwork at all times.

> The Lord your God is in your midst, a mighty one who will save; he will rejoice over you with gladness; he will quiet you by his love; he will exult over you with loud singing. (Zephaniah 3:17)

> These things I have spoken to you, that my joy may be in you, and that your joy may be full. (John 15:11)

> And God saw everything that he had made, and behold, it was very good. And there was evening and there was morning, the sixth day. (Genesis 1:31)

> Bless the Lord, O my soul. O Lord my God, thou art very great; thou art clothed with honour and majesty."

Who coverest thyself with light as with a garment: who stretchest out the heavens like a curtain:
Who layeth the beams of his chambers in the waters: who maketh the clouds his chariot: who walketh upon the wings of the wind:
Who maketh his angels spirits; his ministers a flaming fire:
Who laid the foundations of the earth, that it should not be removed forever.
Thou coveredst it with the deep as with a garment: the waters stood above the mountains.
At thy rebuke they fled; at the voice of thy thunder they hasted away.
They go up by the mountains; they go down by the valleys unto the place which thou hast founded for them.
Thou hast set a bound that they may not pass over; that they turn not again to cover the earth.
He sendeth the springs into the valleys, which run among the hills.
They give drink to every beast of the field: the wild asses quench their thirst.
By them shall the fowls of the heaven have their habitation, which sing among the branches.
He watereth the hills from his chambers: the earth is satisfied with the fruit of thy works.
He causeth the grass to grow for the cattle, and herb for the service of man: that he may bring forth food out of the earth;
And wine that maketh glad the heart of man, and oil to make his face to shine, and bread which strengtheneth man's heart.

The trees of the Lord are full of sap; the cedars of Lebanon, which he hath planted;
Where the birds make their nests: as for the stork, the fir trees are her house.

The high hills are a refuge for the wild goats; and the rocks for the conies.

He appointed the moon for seasons: the sun knoweth his going down.

Thou makest darkness, and it is night: wherein all the beasts of the forest do creep forth.

The young lions roar after their prey, and seek their meat from God.

The sun ariseth, they gather themselves together, and lay them down in their dens.

Man goeth forth unto his work and to his labour until the evening.

O Lord, how manifold are thy works! in wisdom hast thou made them all: the earth is full of thy riches.

So is this great and wide sea, wherein are things creeping innumerable, both small and great beasts.

There go the ships: there is that leviathan, whom thou hast made to play therein.

These wait all upon thee; that thou mayest give them their meat in due season.

That thou givest them they gather: thou openest thine hand, they are filled with good.

Thou hidest thy face, they are troubled: thou takest away their breath, they die, and return to their dust.

Thou sendest forth thy spirit, they are created: and thou renewest the face of the earth.

The glory of the Lord shall endure for ever: the Lord shall rejoice in his works.

He looketh on the earth, and it trembleth: he toucheth the hills, and they smoke.

I will sing unto the Lord as long as I live: I will sing praise to my God while I have my being.

My meditation of him shall be sweet: I will be glad in the Lord.

Let the sinners be consumed out of the earth, and let
the wicked be no more. Bless thou the Lord, O my soul.
Praise ye the Lord. (Psalm 104:1–35 KJV)

LIVING CREATURES ON EARTH

Having fulfilled His pleasures in the firmament and the seas, the
amazing Creator returns back to visit the land with living wonders.
Genesis 1:24–25 states, "And God said, Let the earth bring forth the
living creature after his kind, cattle, and creeping thing, and beast of
the earth after his kind: and it was so. And God made the beast of the
earth after his kind, and cattle after their kind, and everything that
creepeth upon the earth after his kind: and God saw that it was good."
It should be said here that one thing stands out about God: He loves
life. He delights in things that not only are alive but have abundance
of life. John 10:10 says, "I am come that they might have life, and that
they might have it more abundantly."

He is a living and never dying God who is full of life, and everything
within and about Him are overflowing with life. Hence all that emanates
from him are full of life. Nothing sickly, nothing rickety, nothing 99
percent perfected, but full-blown, 100 percent perfected with all it takes
to be all they ought to be. God does not lack any form of resources to
lavish on anything He ever created because He does not have to sweat
to produce them. In fact, he does not require a raw material to bring
into being whatever He desires at any point in time. All He needs to
do is make them be, and they come into being. He can wish them into
being or speak them into being:

> And God said let there be light, and there was light.
> And God called the light day, and it was day.
> And God called the darkness night, and it was night.
> And God said let there be firmament, and it was so.
> And God called the firmament heaven, and it was so.
> And God said let the waters gather, and it was so.
> And God said let dry land appear, and it was so.
> And God called the dry land Earth, and it was so.

And God called the gathered waters seas, and it was so
And God said let the earth bring forth grass, herbs, and
fruit trees, and it was so.
And God said let there be lights in the heavens, and it
was so.

The making and process of creation of everything was done with ease and out of pleasures; hence, they all cannot but enjoy all the pleasures by which they were all created.

God, the Creator, never lacks anything in His abode. He never suffers pains, anguish, hatred, sicknesses, or afflictions, and hence His thought toward His creatures are the same: "For I know the thoughts that I think toward you, sayeth the LORD, thoughts of peace, and not of evil, to give you an expected end" (Jeremiah 29:11).

Woe unto them that call evil good, and good evil; that
put darkness for light, and light for darkness; that put
bitter for sweet, and sweet for bitter! (Isaiah 5:20 KJV)

And now the land is to experience fullness of living creatures by way of cattle, creeping things, and beasts. All were created good as well as in abundance. If the Lord had seen any defect in them, they would not have represented His perfect will, plan, and purpose. In fact, God has wise angels, powerful angels, able angels—by the way, they are all his creatures too—but even though they were able in their capacity to do wonderful things, God never gave the work of creation to any of them. He could have opted to supervise them, but He perhaps considered that their wisdom and skills were not adequate to bring into being His perfect desires. Hence, He decided to do the work by Himself in order to fully satisfy his pleasures.

To whom then will ye liken me, or shall I be equal?
saith the Holy One. Lift up your eyes on high, and
behold who hath created these things, that bringeth out
their host by number: he calleth them all by names by

the greatness of his might, for that he is strong in power; not one faileth. (Isaiah 40:25–26)

Thus saith the LORD, The heaven is my throne, and the earth is my footstool: where is the house that ye build unto me? And where is the place of my rest? For all those things hath mine hand made, and all those things have been, saith the LORD. (Isaiah 66:1–2)

The Land Creatures

A closer look at some of the land creatures attest to the greatness and display of God's pleasure in all of them. Think about the intimidating design of the rhino. The ground is shaky as this animal's heavy weight, exceeding one thousand kilograms, steps out of the corner of a bush! What a massive body with solid protruding horns, and the tough skin can withstand all weather. Here comes the elephant, with specially designed massive ears, massive body, a massive protruding but elegant nose, and sturdy feet with firmness—so firm as firm can be. And with abundance of flesh to spare!

The jungle also displays arrays of powerful yet beautiful and elegant animals to feed the eyes. The lions look regal, golden, and majestic, and they are built in an excellent outfit. Not far away are the tigers beckoning for a fascinating parade with their recognizable dark vertical stripes on orange-brown fur with a lighter underside. How about the leopard or the jaguar? Oh, what about the other one with an extremely elongated neck, which can be up to almost eight feet in length? It is the giraffe, glowing with coated skin patterns. What a God of great variety and abundance of wisdom to make all these tall, thin, big, small, light-colored, dark-spotted, and huge creatures, and yet He is not running out of ideas and beauty fashions to display on all of them.

The tiny ones are not left out; none of them is devoid of beauties and colossal designs in outlook. The pygmy rabbit, marmoset, Etruscan Shrew, speckled Padloper tortoise, some frogs. It is nothing short of delight and great excitement to watch all these animals run, play, eat, sleep, reproduce, and carry out amazing activities.

What an amazing pleasure to watch these animals run at their best.

Ostrich: 70km/h (43 mph)
Serval: 70 km/h (43 mph)
Dog: 70 km/h (43 mph)
Horse: 76 km/h (44 mph)
Hare: 80 km/h (50 mph)
Mountain lion: 80 km/h (50 mph)
Jaguar: 80 km/h (50 mph)
Caracal: 80 km/h (50 mph)
Lion: 80 km/h (50 mph)
Pronghorn: 85 km/h (53 mph)
True antelopes and impala: up to 88 km/h (55 mph)
Cheetah: at least 103km/h (64 mph)

O LORD, how manifold are thy works! In wisdom hast thou made them all: the earth is full of thy riches. (Psalm 104:24)

Creeping Things

The masterful Creator found room for innumerable snakes, worms, caterpillars, termites, ants, and others. None of these creatures is debased by any standard. A thorough study of each of them magnifies the creative prowess of God. So much diligence and wisdom is expended on them, thereby making the significance of all creatures notable.

Here is an example of such an amazing thought of God toward the ants just like any of other His creatures. Solomon, who was the wisest king in his generation, could not withdraw his gaze and amazement at the wonders of God, even in ordinary ants.

Go to the ant, thou sluggard; consider her ways, and be wise:
Which having no guide, overseer, or ruler,
Provideth her meat in the summer, and gathereth her food in the harvest. (Proverbs 6:6–7)

> There be four things which are little upon the earth,
> but they are exceeding wise:
>
> The ants are a people not strong, yet they prepare their
> meat in the summer;
> The conies are but a feeble folk, yet make they their
> houses in the rocks;
> The locusts have no king, yet go they forth all of them
> by bands;
> The spider taketh hold with her hands, and is in kings'
> palaces. (Proverbs 30:34–28)

How fascinating it will be to follow through with the ants and the spiders while on duty in all seasons. How exiting! How amazing! And at the end of it all, the stamp of God's goodness will be confirmed to be absolutely legal on them, thereby fulfilling all His pleasures without any objections.

If those tiny objects could speak out, you'll hear them loud and clear saying they carry out all those activities with pleasures in their natural habitats just in like manner as the wild animals have their pleasures in the jungle. All the creatures in the sea will also be praising God for the abundance of water available to them to carry out their activities with pleasure. The flying objects are also flapping their wings for the pleasure of the free firmament.

The Creator is boundless. He is present in every place and shows off by the magnificence of His handiwork. He calls himself "I AM that I AM" to signify to all his creatures the power of His dominion over all things, the source of His power, and His eternal nature: I AM. He is the self-sufficient, self-sustaining God who was, who is, and who will be forever.

> Because that which may be known of God is manifest in
> them; for God hath shewed it unto them. For the invisible
> things of him from the creation of the world are clearly
> seen, being understood by the things that are made, even
> his eternal power and Godhead. (Romans 1:19–20)

It was in the light of this awesomeness and out of the abundance of His creative power that He decided to crown His pleasures with the creation of the most magnificent of all of His creatures under heaven called man. Here is a glimpse of the making.

> I will praise thee; for I am fearfully and wonderfully made: marvelous are thy works; and that my soul knoweth right well.
>
> My substance was not hid from thee, when I was made in secret, and curiously wrought in the lowest parts of the earth.
>
> Thine eyes did see my substance, yet being unperfect; and in thy book all my members were written, which in continuance were fashioned, when as yet there was none of them.
>
> How precious also are thy thoughts unto me, O God! How great is the sum of them!
>
> If I should count them, they are more in number than the sand: when I awake, I am still with thee. (Psalm 139:14–18)

Something that was "fearfully and wonderfully made" took the great deal of God's attention. Anything that takes anyone's attention is an object of great interest and delight. The end product must meet the desires and pleasure of the maker. If the creatures earlier produced by the almighty Creator met this criteria, much more is the very crown of His creation under the heavens: man.

> And God said, Let us make man in our image, after our likeness: and let them have dominion over the fish of the sea, and over the fowl of the air, and over the cattle, and over all the earth, and over every creeping thing that creepeth upon the earth.

So God created man in his own image, in the image of God created he him; male and female created he them.

And God blessed them, and God said unto them, be fruitful, and multiply, and replenish the earth, and subdue it: and have dominion over the fish of the sea, and over the fowl of the air, and over every living thing that moveth upon the earth.

And God said, Behold, I have given you every herb bearing seed, which is upon the face of all the earth, and every tree, in the which is the fruit of a tree yielding seed; to you it shall be for meat.

And to every beast of the earth, and to every fowl of the air, and to everything that creepeth upon the earth, wherein there is life, I have given every green herb for meat: and it was so.

And God saw everything that he had made, and, behold, it was very good. And the evening and the morning were the sixth day. (Genesis 1:26–31; emphasis added)

Man

The creation of man can unequivocally be described as the utmost object of God's pleasure. The tone of God's statement doubtless reflects this: "And God said, Let us make man in our image, after our likeness: and let them have dominion."

1. The invitation—"let us"—that was not referenced at the beginning of all other creatures came out loud and clear at this juncture. That was an indication of something higher, something loftier, and something that must have taken more joy, more delight, more inspiration, and greater and higher expectations in respect to excellence.

2. "In our image." Complete identification with this creature unlike others before now. This special creature was to have all the features and qualities in God manifested in him. This was certainly an expression of affection.

An expression of delight.
An expression of elevation.
An expression of great quality
An expression of special love.
An expression of divine ownership.
An expression of special identity.
An expression of dignity.
An expression of glorification.
An expression of immortality.
An expression of divine attachment.
An expression of unconditional partnership.
An expression of unconditional fellowship.
An expression of utmost pleasure.

3. "Let them have dominion." Authority over the hitherto creatures conferred on man.
Little wonder the Psalmist says,

O Lord, our Lord, how excellent is thy name in all the earth! Who hast set thy glory above the heavens.

Out of the mouth of babes and sucklings hast thou ordained strength because of thine enemies, that thou mightest still the enemy and the avenger.

When I consider thy heavens, the work of thy fingers, the moon and the stars, which thou hast ordained;

What is man, that thou art mindful of him? and the son of man, that thou visitest him?

For thou hast made him a little lower than the angels, and hast crowned him with glory and honour.

Thou madest him to have dominion over the works of thy hands; thou hast put all things under his feet:

All sheep and oxen, yea, and the beasts of the field;

The fowl of the air, and the fish of the sea, and whatsoever passeth through the paths of the seas.

O Lord our Lord, how excellent is thy name in all the earth! (Psalm 8:1–9 KJV)

This is nothing but the outpouring of God's great pleasures upon this being called man. In fact, Proverbs 8:25–31 (emphasis added) puts it plainly:

Before the mountains were settled, before the hills was I brought forth:

While as yet he had not made the earth, nor the fields, nor the highest part of the dust of the world.

When he prepared the heavens, I was there: when he set a compass upon the face of the depth:

When he established the clouds above: when he strengthened the fountains of the deep:

When he gave to the sea his decree, that the waters should not pass his commandment: when he appointed the foundations of the earth:

Then I was by him, as one brought up with him: and I was daily his delight, rejoicing always before him;

Rejoicing in the habitable part of his earth; and my delights were with the sons of men.

The love of God for man, among all His creatures, is amazingly unique. He lavished him with all resources, all endowments, and riches in wisdom, knowledge and understanding, beauty, grace, creative power, and the like. The long and short of it is that it was upon man God so lavished His pleasures by making him so special. He literally crowned man as a mini God to rule and reign.

Man was in the image and likeness of the Creator. The very thought of God with respect to man originally was to have largely all his core attributes. "For we are members of His body, of His flesh and of His bones" (Ephesians 5:20).

1. Man was designed to be immortal from the day of creation, with all the resources enjoyed to continuously multiply rather than decrease. "Make man in our image, after our likeness."(Genesis 1:26a) Living immortally with no problems, no lack, no devil, no sicknesses, no sin, no harm, no fear, no intimidation, no death—this was pleasure par excellence.

2. Invincible, never to be defeated: "And God blessed them, and God said unto them, Be fruitful, and multiply, and replenish the earth, and subdue it."(Genesis 1:28a).

3. To be holy and pure, answerable only to the Maker.

4. Covered with the glory of God, his Maker: "This people have I formed for myself; they shall shew forth my praise" (Isaiah 43:21).

5. Ever to be in a state of goodness: "And God saw everything that he had made, and, behold, it was very good."(Genesis 1:31a)

6. Man was meant to enjoy abundance beyond measure forever.

> And God blessed them, and God said unto them,
> Be fruitful, and multiply, and replenish the earth,
> and subdue it: and have dominion over the fish of
> the sea, and over the fowl of the air, and over every
> living thing that moveth upon the earth.

> And God said, Behold, I have given you every herb
> bearing seed, which is upon the face of all the earth,
> and every tree, in the which is the fruit of a tree
> yielding seed; to you it shall be for meat.
>
> And to every beast of the earth, and to every fowl
> of the air, and to everything that creepeth upon the
> earth, wherein there is life, I have given every green
> herb for meat: and it was so.(Genesis 1:29-30).

7. Nothing was ever meant to be harmful to him from the land,
   the seas, or the firmament. All were meant to serve him. "And
   Adam gave names to all cattle, and to the fowl of the air, and
   to every beast of the field" (Genesis 2:20).
8. Man was to have fellowship with God, the Maker, forever: "And
   they heard the voice of the Lord God walking in the garden in
   the cool of the day" (Genesis 3:8a). "And the Lord God called
   to Adam, and said unto him, Where art thou?"(Genesis 3:9)
   Imagine having fellowship with the all in all God. The Bible
   says

> Their sorrows shall be multiplied that hasten after
> another god: their drink offerings of blood will I
> not offer, nor take up their names into my lips. The
> Lord is the portion of mine inheritance and of my
> cup: thou maintainest my lot. The lines are fallen
> unto me in pleasant places; yea, I have a goodly
> heritage.(Psalm 16:4-6)
>
> Thou wilt shew me the path of life: in thy presence
> is *fullness of joy*; at thy right hand there are *pleasures
> for evermore.*(Psalm 16:11; emphasis added)

9. Man was to be secured and comforted on every side:

> I will lift up mine eyes unto the hills, from whence
> cometh my help.

My help cometh from the Lord, which made heaven and earth.

He will not suffer thy foot to be moved: he that keepeth thee will not slumber.

Behold, he that keepeth Israel shall neither slumber nor sleep.

The Lord is thy keeper: the Lord is thy shade upon thy right hand.

The sun shall not smite thee by day, nor the moon by night.

The Lord shall preserve thee from all evil: he shall preserve thy soul.

The Lord shall preserve thy going out and thy coming in from this time forth, and even for evermore. (Psalm 121:1–8 KJV)

10. Man was created to be a showcase of God's glory.

This people have I formed for myself; they shall shew forth my praise. (Isaiah 43:21)

But ye are a chosen generation, a royal priesthood, an holy nation, a peculiar people; that ye should shew forth the praises of him who hath called you out of darkness into his marvelous light. (1 Peter 2:9)

11. Man was created to enjoy all the goodness of His maker.

The Lord is my shepherd; I shall not want.

He maketh me to lie down in green pastures: he leadeth me beside the still waters.

He restoreth my soul: he leadeth me in the paths of righteousness for his name's sake.

Surely goodness and mercy shall follow me all the
days of my life: and I will dwell in the house of the
Lord forever. (Psalm 23:1–3, 5–6)

12. Man was created with very special privileges.

And the LORD God formed man of the dust of the
ground, and breathed into his nostrils the breath
of life; and man became a living soul.(Genesis 2:7).

And God blessed them, and God said unto them,
Be fruitful, and multiply, and replenish the earth,
and subdue it: and have dominion over the fish of
the sea, and over the fowl of the air, and over every
living thing that moveth upon the earth. (Genesis
1:28)

The summary of God's original desire for man and all is made
manifest in Psalms 36:8, "They shall be abundantly satisfied with the
fatness of thy house; and thou shalt make them drink of the river of thy
pleasures." Why? For the simple reason that all things were designed
for pleasures.

Thou art worthy, O Lord, to receive glory and honor
and power: for thou hast created all things, and for thy
pleasure they are and were created. ('Revelation 4:11)

THE PLEASURES IN
THE GARDEN

Let's begin from the Garden of Eden. Imagine entering the gates of the garden to check in as a resident. The song that might readily come to mind is

> I will enter His gates with thanksgiving in my heart
> I will enter His court with praise
> I will say this is the Day that the Lord has made
> I will rejoice for He has made me glad.
> - Maranathan singers, 1998

This is backed up by the sweet Psalmist in Psalms 100:4, "Enter into his gates with thanksgiving, and into his courts with praise: be thankful unto him, and bless his name."

While by the gate of the Garden of Eden, one could imagine the enormity of the supply therein by the mere name. It was called Eden: a place or state of great happiness, an unspoiled paradise. Oh, my! It's like heaven come down in a mini form. Wait a moment—one of the seven ancient wonders on earth is said to be the Hanging Gardens in Babylon, built between 605 and 562 BC. The description of this man-made garden is said to be likened to rivers of pleasures garnished with "remarkable feat of engineering with an ascending series of tiered gardens containing a wide variety of trees, shrubs, and vines, resembling a large green mountain constructed of mud bricks."(Hanging Gardens of Babylon–Wikipedia).

If a man-made garden could be one of the seven ancient wonders of the world, it cannot be fathomed how gorgeous, glorious, tasteful, beautiful, and marvelous the garden made by the wise master designer of all things to the most precise and perfection will look like. Bible says in Ecclesiastes 3:14, "I know that, whatsoever God doeth, it shall be forever: nothing can be put to it, nor any thing taken from it: and God doeth it, that men should fear before him."

Therefore, approaching the gate of the Garden of Eden brings forth a question: why the word *Garden*?

1. The first thing that might come to mind is beauty. Anything beautiful is attractive, admirable, and good for well-being and therefore is appealing to the point of producing pleasure.
2. Another feature expected will be a variety of trees, flowers, moving objects, and shelters.
3. There is calmness and a peaceful environment.
4. It is artistically designed.
5. It is an aesthetically gorgeous environment.
6. Everything therein speaks volumes to the admiration of everyone.
7. The landscape is fantastically attractive.
8. It is a vibrant landscape, perhaps with walls, paths, terraces, pools, and similar elements, that will create a strong structure and year-round attractiveness.

It is common knowledge that formal gardens in the Western tradition are characterized by the following.

• Bilateral symmetry: one side of the garden is the mirror image of the other. Hardscape, plant material, and the shape of the garden beds are similar on either side of an axis so that the appearance of perfect balance is created. If there is a tall tree on one side of the garden, there will be a similar tree in the same position on the other side of the garden.

- Dominant hardscape with walls, paths, terraces, pools, and similar elements creating a strong structure and year-round attractiveness.
- Perfect proportions with hedges, paths, flower beds, walls, and other garden features in proportion to each other to create a restful, peaceful, enduring ambiance that emphasizes a control over the natural environment.
- Repetition of hardscape elements and plant material to provide rhythm and strong balance.
- Geometric shapes with strong emphasis on right angles and rectangular forms.
- Straight paths.
- Man-made, level topography.
- Clipped shrubs, hedges, and lawn with everything appearing to be in its place and under complete control.
- Classical garden ornaments such as statues, urns, and topiaries.
- Surrounded by a visual barrier such as a wall, clipped hedge, or dramatic elevation change of the ground to give it a clear separation from the surrounding natural landscape.

With the symbolic name *Garden of Eden* in mind, the abundantly furnished abode of the first man must have been dazzling and gloriously beautiful. More so, the almighty God was the builder of the place. The Creator made available all that man was ever going to need ready before ever creating him. In fact, the garden is often referred to as the Garden of God, signifying how dignifying it must have been.

Let's not forget that the place was even glorious enough for God to come down from heaven to fellowship there with Adam. Solomon says in 1 Kings 8:27, "But will God indeed dwell on the earth? behold, the heaven and heaven of heavens cannot contain thee; how much less this house that I have builded?"

For God to find the garden attractive enough to visit, it must have met a heavenly standard by no small means. Only very rich men in this world have very well designed and furnished gardens. Come to think of it, God has all things available unto Him both visible and invisible, and He always puts His best to anything He does and cannot be rivaled because all His works are perfect! This garden therefore must have been designed to be like heaven on earth. It was made and fully equipped for the maximum pleasure of the residents.

> And the LORD God planted a garden eastward in Eden; and there he put the man whom he had formed.

> And out of the ground made the LORD God to grow every tree that is pleasant to the sight, and good for food; the tree of life also in the midst of the garden, and the tree of knowledge of good and evil.

> And a river went out of Eden to water the garden; and from thence it was parted, and became into four heads.

> The name of the first is Pison: that is it which compasseth the whole land of Havilah, where there is gold;

> And the gold of that land is good: there is bdellium and the onyx stone.

> And the name of the second river is Gihon: the same is it that compasseth the whole land of Ethiopia.

> And the name of the third river is Hiddekel: that is it which goeth toward the east of Assyria. And the fourth river is Euphrates.

> And the LORD God took the man, and put him into the Garden of Eden to dress it and to keep it. (Genesis 2:8–15)

Here could be otherwise called the Garden of Pleasures because we are introduced to the Garden thus: the LORD God making every tree that was pleasant to the sight and good for food. All the millions of trees, flowers, shrubs, and grasses were pleasant to the eyes. The nature of the food was the same. Therefore, the rivers, whatever shelter, the animals, the hills and valleys, the flying objects, and the crawling or swimming ones would have fit into the same description. All was pleasant to the eyes, with good feelings, good tastes, and good sights. Everything in the garden was glamorous.

The watering of the garden must have been of great delight for all-purpose usage. He did not need to sweat to do the watering. There was provision to make the trees and the grass ever green. There was a divine sprinkler system, perhaps with a pleasant sound when the plants were being watered. Everything must have been to precision as well as right on time. The flow of the river on different paths must have been another wonderful thing to gaze upon. Perhaps while in the garden at the cool of the day, Adam looked faraway as to how endlessly the River Pison was flowing, and so was River Gihon, River Hiddekel, and last of all River Euphrates. What a lovely landscape this must have been.

Doubtless that mineral resources in the rivers, in the land, and all around were some of the precious things at the reach of the only man ever created, for he was given control over the whole earth.

There was the mention of one of the costliest mineral resources in the history of humankind to this present day: "And the gold of that land is good" (Genesis 2:12). Why in the world was there mention of good gold? It's a special treasure and a symbol of wealth and perfection. It is a point of reference to the fact that everything within and without the garden was in perfect condition without anything to add or subtract. Everywhere had the touch of God, who is masterful and perfect in all His doings. None can improve upon what He has done or created. Hence, everything was designed for pleasure!

Everything Adam tasted, everything Adam used, everything Adam felt (Just like God after all creations), and everything Adam saw were "very good" without any exception. Adam originally had the mind and the spirit of God: "And the LORD God formed man of the dust of the ground, and breathed into his nostrils the breath of life; and man became a living soul" (Genesis 2:7). He was therefore pleasured by everything within and around him. They were all created for his pleasures too. Moreover, all the things that God created received nothing short of His maximum blessings.

The blessing of the LORD, it maketh rich, and he addeth no sorrow with it. (Proverbs 10:22)

And the LORD met Balaam, and put a word in his mouth, and said, Go again unto Balak, and say thus.

And when he came to him, behold, he stood by his burnt offering, and the princes of Moab with him. And Balak said unto him, What hath the LORD spoken?

And he took up his parable, and said, Rise up, Balak, and hear; hearken unto me, thou son of Zippor:

God is not a man that he should lie; neither the son of man that he should repent: hath he said, and shall he not do it? or hath he spoken, and shall he not make it good?

Behold, I have received commandment to bless: and he hath blessed; and I cannot reverse it. (Numbers 23:16–19)

Blessings are meant to be enjoyed. Blessings make for joy, happiness, delight, and celebrations. Blessings are good stuff, for good feelings and glory to the source of the blessings (which is primarily God).

What gift of love could I offer to a King?
What weight or worth could be held within my offering?
When He alone is worthy

A glory song is inscribed upon my heart
This treasure held in an alabaster jar I break
To bring Him all the glory

Praise God from whom all blessings flow
Praise Him all creatures here below
...

—Brooke Ligertwood

One would have thought because everything God has made for man to enjoy was already more than enough in the garden, and because the blessings of fruitfulness and dominion were far beyond imaginations, all was set. Rather, the Creator saw a need to do more. There was not a single complaint from Adam of any lack, any discomfort, any weakness, any emotional trauma, any inadequacy, or any vacancy or loophole. But the gracious God discovered and desired to add more to the already overwhelming blessings bestowed on Adam and other creatures with him. This time around, God decided to add to the pleasures already being enjoyed by Adam.

> And Adam gave names to all cattle, and to the fowl of the air, and to every beast of the field; but for Adam there was not found an help meet for him.

> And the LORD God caused a deep sleep to fall upon Adam, and he slept: and he took one of his ribs, and closed up the flesh instead thereof;

> And the rib, which the LORD God had taken from man, made he a woman, and brought her unto the man. (Genesis 1:20–22)

When Eve manifested through the amazing miracle of the Creator and was brought to Adam, it created a feeling of indescribable deeper satisfaction, love, emotional attachment, higher sense of gratitude, delight of a higher magnitude, and pleasure on a higher and deeper level that was hitherto ever experienced. Hence the statement that oozed out of Adam described it all when he suddenly saw a package of beauty from head to the toes. "And Adam said, this is now bone of my bones, and flesh of my flesh: she shall be called Woman, because she was taken out of Man" (Genesis 2:23).

It can therefore be concluded that everything in the garden and the manifestation of Eve was well pleasing as an additional blessings to Adam. All these were originally designed for the good of all creatures. Everything that was supposed to be an offshoot, from the garden to the ends of the earth, was designed to be harmoniously in line with the thoughts of the Creator forever.

> So God created man in his own image, in the image of God created he him; male and female created he them. And God blessed them, and God said unto them, be fruitful, and multiply, and replenish the earth, and subdue it: and have dominion over the fish of the sea, and over the fowl of the air, and over every living thing that moveth upon the earth. (Genesis 1:27–28)

They were to be fruitful and multiply and replenish the earth with blessings, not burdens.
They were to be fruitful and multiply and replenish the earth with joy, not sorrows.
They were to be fruitful and multiply and replenish the earth with abundance, not lack.
They were to be fruitful and multiply and replenish the earth with peace, not wars.
They were to be fruitful and multiply and replenish the earth with health, not sicknesses.
They were to be fruitful and multiply and replenish the earth with wisdom, not foolishness.
They were to be fruitful and multiply and replenish the earth with fellowship, not hostility.
They were to be fruitful and multiply and replenish the earth to preserve, not destroy.
They were to be fruitful and multiply and replenish the earth with godliness, not evil.
They were to be fruitful and multiply and replenish the earth with coexistence, not feuding.
They were to be fruitful and multiply and replenish the earth with freedom, not bondage.
They were to be fruitful and multiply and replenish the earth with prosperity, not poverty.

They were to be fruitful and multiply and
replenish the earth with comfort, not afflictions.
They were to be fruitful and multiply and
replenish the earth with well-being, not distress.
They were to be fruitful and multiply and
replenish the earth with pleasure, not pains.
They were to be fruitful and multiply and
replenish the earth with life, not death.
They were to be fruitful and multiply and replenish
the earth with goodness, not wickedness.
They were to be fruitful and multiply and
replenish the earth with peace, not wars.
They were to be fruitful and multiply and
replenish the earth with bliss, not oppression.

But wait a minute—was Adam not supposed to expend energy in pains and in agony? For it is written, "And the LORD God took the man, and put him into the Garden of Eden to dress it and to keep it" (Genesis 2:15). I beg to submit that it was all in pleasure and with pleasure too.

God's way has always been this. "Then he answered and spake unto me, saying, this is the word of the Lord unto Zerubbabel, saying, not by might, nor by power, but by my spirit, saith the Lord of hosts" (Zechariah 4:6 KJV).

Jesus said, "For My Yoke is easy, and my burden is light" (Matthew 11:30 KJV).

God places a curse in Deuteronomy 28:47, "Because thou servedst not the LORD thy God with joyfulness, and with gladness of heart, for the abundance of all things."

Also, "to dress it and to keep" was later changed to the following.

And unto Adam he said, Because thou hast hearkened
unto the voice of thy wife, and hast eaten of the tree,
of which I commanded thee, saying, Thou shalt not eat

of it: cursed is the ground for thy sake; in sorrow shalt thou eat of it all the days of thy life;

Thorns also and thistles shall it bring forth to thee; and thou shalt eat the herb of the field;

In the sweat of thy face shalt thou eat bread, till thou return unto the ground; for out of it wast thou taken: for dust thou art, and unto dust shalt thou return.

Therefore the LORD God sent him forth from the Garden of Eden, to till the ground from whence he was taken. (Genesis 3:17–23)

The tilling, sorrow, and sweating was not the original plan of the Creator for Adam or humanity as a whole. The original dressing and the keeping by Adam before the era of sin would have been effortless, delightful, joyful, burden free, and stress free. It's like exercising a gift of God with so much joy and gladness. It would have been like a fish in the river or a bird flying in the air.

Adam was not only to enjoy all the variety of things put under his dominion; he was also to enjoy his wife with great pleasure, and of course vice versa.

Adam and His Wife

Adam and Eve were designed to have pleasures.

Drink waters out of thine own cistern, and running waters out of thine own well.

Let thy fountains be dispersed abroad, and rivers of waters in the streets.

Let them be only thine own, and not strangers' with thee.

Let thy fountain be blessed: and rejoice with the wife of thy youth.

Let her be as the loving hind and pleasant roe; let her breasts satisfy thee at all times; and be thou ravished always with her love. (Proverbs 5:15–19)

And Adam said, this is now bone of my bones, and flesh of my flesh: she shall be called Woman, because she was taken out of Man.

Therefore shall a man leave his father and his mother, and shall cleave unto his wife: and they shall be one flesh.

And they were both naked, the man and his wife, and were not ashamed. (Genesis 2:23–25)

Two are better than one; because they have a good reward for their labour.

For if they fall, the one will lift up his fellow: but woe to him that is alone when he falleth; for he hath not another to help him up.

Again, if two lie together, then they have heat: but how can one be warm alone? (Ecclesiastes 4:9–12 KJV)

Who can find a virtuous woman? For her price is far above rubies.

The heart of her husband doth safely trust in her, so that he shall have no need of spoil.

She will do him good and not evil all the days of her life. (Proverbs 31:10–12)

And Adam gave names to all cattle, and to the fowl of the air, and to every beast of the field; but for Adam there was not found a **help meet** for him. (Genesis 2:20).

Adam, Eve, and Children

Adam, Eve, and children were designed to have happy, joyous, delightful, pleasurable, and fruitful lives. The production of babies was meant to be without pains, pangs, and sorrows in the original plan. In fact, the Bible says in Psalm 126:3–5, "Lo, children are an heritage of the LORD: and the fruit of the womb is his reward. As arrows are in the hand of a mighty man; so are children of the youth. Happy is the man that hath his quiver full of them: they shall not be ashamed, but they shall speak with the enemies in the gate."

> So God created man in his own image, in the image of God created he him; male and female created he them. And God blessed them, and God said unto them, be fruitful, and multiply, and replenish the earth. (Genesis 1:27–28)

> Behold, I and the children whom the LORD hath given me are for signs and for wonders in Israel from the LORD of hosts, which dwelleth in mount Zion. (Isaiah 8:18)

> Thy wife shall be as a fruitful vine by the sides of thine house: thy children like olive plants round about thy table. (Psalm 128:3)

> And they brought young children to him, that he should touch them: and his disciples rebuked those that brought them.

But when Jesus saw it, he was much displeased, and said unto them, Suffer the little children to come unto me, and forbid them not: for of such is the kingdom of God.

Verily I say unto you, whosoever shall not receive the kingdom of God as a little child, he shall not enter therein.

And he took them up in his arms, put his hands upon them, and blessed them. (Mark 10:13–16)

The Family and the Presence of God

The most glorious, most delightful, most joyful, most satisfying, most peaceful, and most adorable was the very presence of God with the family of Adam. The presence of God is the highest of all pleasures.

"Thou wilt shew me the path of life: in thy presence is fullness of joy; at thy right hand there are pleasures for evermore" (Psalm 16:11 KJV).

Blessed is the man whom thou choosest, and causest to approach unto thee, that he may dwell in thy courts: we shall be satisfied with the goodness of thy house, even of thy holy temple. (Psalm 65:4)

Now the Lord is that Spirit: and where the Spirit of the Lord is, there is liberty. (2 Corinthians 3:17)

Adam's Family and Privileges

Adam and his family were bestowed with the highest of all privileges and authority over all things under the heaven.

- First-class access to all the resources on earth.
- First-class access to God the Creator.

- First-class access over all the affairs of the kingdom of this whole world.
- First-class attention for any need, direct from the Creator.
- First-class role model responsibilities.
- First-class taste of everything in their original states.

The state of the garden and the inhabitants is beyond description. Everything was pure and original.

Feelings were pure and original.
Food of diverse kinds were pure and original.
Love was pure and original.
Relationships were pure and original.
Fellowship with God was pure and original.
Desires were pure and original.
Landscapes were perfect and original.
Freshness of all things was pure and original.
Weather was perfectly pure and original.

When the night dawned to take a sleep, what delight it was to have a kind of sleep in a perfect environment and in a peaceful and perfect state of mind, to crown such a sleep with dreams of heavenly stuff, visitation of God and the angels descending and ascending like Jacob's in Genesis 28:10–14.

And Jacob went out from Beersheba, and went toward Haran.

And he lighted upon a certain place, and tarried there all night, because the sun was set; and he took of the stones of that place, and put them for his pillows, and lay down in that place to sleep.

And he dreamed, and behold a ladder set up on the earth, and the top of it reached to heaven: and behold the angels of God ascending and descending on it.

And, behold, the LORD stood above it, and said, I am the LORD God of Abraham thy father, and the God of Isaac: the land whereon thou liest, to thee will I give it, and to thy seed;

And thy seed shall be as the dust of the earth, and thou shalt spread abroad to the west, and to the east, and to the north, and to the south: and in thee and in thy seed shall all the families of the earth be blessed.

Neither day nor night would have been filled with the abundance of the goodness of the good Creator. For such was everything designed by the Creator. Adam's family could wake up each morning and must have sung something close to Lamentations 3:22–23 (ESV).

The steadfast love of the Lord never ceases;
his mercies never come to an end;
they are new every morning;
great is your faithfulness.

As the sun shines upon them to usher them in a new day, they could shout out to the Lord for all His goodness and mercies.

Praise ye the Lord. Praise, O ye servants of the Lord, praise the name of the Lord.

Blessed be the name of the Lord from this time forth and for evermore.

From the rising of the sun unto the going down of the same the Lord's name is to be praised.

The Lord is high above all nations, and his glory above the heavens.

Who is like unto the Lord our God, who dwelleth on high,

Who humbleth himself to behold the things that are in heaven, and in the earth! (Psalm 113:1-6 KJV)

What If ...

Here are some postulations in respect to the continuity of God's designed pleasures for His creatures.

1. What if there was no devil?
2. What if there was no tempter or temptation?
3. What if Eve and Adam had overcome the temptation?
4. What if there was no curse from God, the Creator?

Well, you can be sure that the original plan and purpose of the Creator would have continued forever.

> No death.
> No disaster.
> No pain.
> No panic
> No sorrow.
> No sickness.
> No suffering.
> No fear.
> No falling.
> No failing.
> No fainting.
> No falsehood.
> No lack.
> No loss.
> No limitations.

The scriptures would have been fulfilled as penned down in Job 36:11, "If they obey and serve him, they shall spend their days in prosperity, and their years in pleasures."

The very prototype of life with God's presence was the picture painted before the Israelites of old and the Promised Land. The promises and the grand intentions of God were to bring heaven down for the chosen people, similar to the Garden of Eden. However, this was still significantly limited in that nothing could be compared with the original.

A quick look at the well-being of the Israelites as promised by God will convince us of the goodness and care of God for His creatures, though in a limited form.

Canaan was to be "the *land which I had given them, flowing with milk and honey, which is the glory of all lands" (Ezekiel 20:15).* Canaan was to be full of abundance all year round.

> For the land, whither thou goest in to possess it, is not as the land of Egypt, from whence ye came out, where thou sowedst thy seed, and wateredst it with thy foot, as a garden of herbs:
>
> But the land, whither ye go to possess it, is a land of hills and valleys, and drinketh water of the rain of heaven:
>
> A land which the Lord thy God careth for: the eyes of the Lord thy God are always upon it, from the beginning of the year even unto the end of the year.
>
> And it shall come to pass, if ye shall hearken diligently unto my commandments which I command you this day, to love the Lord your God, and to serve him with all your heart and with all your soul,
>
> That I will give you the rain of your land in his due season, the first rain and the latter rain, that thou mayest gather in thy corn, and thy wine, and thine oil.
>
> And I will send grass in thy fields for thy cattle, that thou mayest eat and be full.(Deuteronomy 10:10-15).

Wow! Ponder over living an abundant live in the Promised Land. They were even assured of rest and peace all around.

> Therefore it shall be, when the LORD thy God hath given thee rest from all thine enemies round about, in the land which the LORD thy God giveth thee for an inheritance to possess it, that thou shalt blot out the remembrance of Amalek from under heaven; thou shalt not forget it. (Deuteronomy 25:19)

Not only was the Promised Land supposed to be a land of peace and abundance with the presence of God, but unimaginable other promises were added. What else can one term the following but pleasures?

> And it shall come to pass, if thou shalt hearken diligently unto the voice of the Lord thy God, to observe and to do all his commandments which I command thee this day, that the Lord thy God will set thee on high above all nations of the earth:

> And all these blessings shall come on thee, and overtake thee, if thou shalt hearken unto the voice of the Lord thy God.

> Blessed shalt thou be in the city, and blessed shalt thou be in the field.

> Blessed shall be the fruit of thy body, and the fruit of thy ground, and the fruit of thy cattle, the increase of thy kine, and the flocks of thy sheep.

> Blessed shall be thy basket and thy store.

> Blessed shalt thou be when thou comest in, and blessed shalt thou be when thou goest out.

The Lord shall cause thine enemies that rise up against thee to be smitten before thy face: they shall come out against thee one way, and flee before thee seven ways.

The Lord shall command the blessing upon thee in thy storehouses, and in all that thou settest thine hand unto; and he shall bless thee in the land which the Lord thy God giveth thee.

The Lord shall establish thee an holy people unto himself, as he hath sworn unto thee, if thou shalt keep the commandments of the Lord thy God, and walk in his ways.

And all people of the earth shall see that thou art called by the name of the Lord; and they shall be afraid of thee.

And the Lord shall make thee plenteous in goods, in the fruit of thy body, and in the fruit of thy cattle, and in the fruit of thy ground, in the land which the Lord sware unto thy fathers to give thee.

The Lord shall open unto thee his good treasure, the heaven to give the rain unto thy land in his season, and to bless all the work of thine hand: and thou shalt lend unto many nations, and thou shalt not borrow.

And the Lord shall make thee the head, and not the tail; and thou shalt be above only, and thou shalt not be beneath; if that thou hearken unto the commandments of the Lord thy God, which I command thee this day, to observe and to do them. (Deuteronomy 28:1-14 KJV)

The creatures could not ask for more of the pleasures and the goodness of God toward them than all these wonderful things. But the summary of the crown of all the lofty promises is in Deuteronomy 11:21 (KJV).

That your days may be multiplied, and the days of your children, in the land which the Lord sware unto your fathers to give them, as the days of heaven upon the earth.

Four

———— ✑ ————

ULTIMATE DESIRE OF GOD, THE CREATOR

Who God is determines what His desires are.

Let's find out what the scriptures say about Him and His ultimate desires about everything, especially regarding His creatures. It is of paramount and great significance to bear in mind that ""For as he thinketh in his heart, so is he" (Proverbs 23:7 KJV). "A good man out of the good treasure of his heart bringeth forth that which is good; and an evil man out of the evil treasure of his heart bringeth forth that which is evil: for of the abundance of the heart his mouth speaketh" (Luke 6:45).

The Bible affirms that God is good.

> And Jesus said unto him, Why callest thou me good?
> None is good, save one, that is, God. (Luke 18:19)
>
> Oh, taste and see that the Lord is good;
> blessed is the man who trusts in Him!
> Oh, fear the Lord, you His saints!
> There is no want to those who fear Him.
> The young lions lack and suffer hunger;
> But those who seek the Lord shall not lack any good
> thing.(Psalm 34:8–10)

For the Lord God is a sun and shield: the Lord will give grace and glory: no good thing will he withhold from them that walk uprightly. (Psalm 84:11)

O give thanks unto the LORD, for he is good: for his mercy endureth forever. (Psalm 107:1)

God is good to all: and his tender mercies are over all his works. All thy works shall praise thee, O LORD; and thy saints shall bless thee. (Psalm 145:9–10)

In the light of the above infallible scriptures, God, the Creator of all things, is absolutely good. Good things proceed from someone who is good. It therefore confirms that all that God created proceeded out of Him as only being good. He confirmed about everything He created by the word of His mouth, saying they were "very good." It therefore goes without saying that the ultimate desires of the Creator for all His creatures were nothing but good.

All thy works shall praise thee, O Lord; and thy saints shall bless thee.

They shall speak of the glory of thy kingdom, and talk of thy power;

To make known to the sons of men his mighty acts, and the glorious majesty of his kingdom.

Thy kingdom is an everlasting kingdom, and thy dominion endureth throughout all generations. (Psalm 145:10–13)

The powerful emphasis of the scriptures that all His works shall praise Him is a notion to attest to the goodness and excellence of all the creatures of God leading to praises and nothing short of it at every level. This was the very original delight of God for all His creatures. He created them for His pleasure. Doubtless, the pleasures of God are without any form of evil because in Him, there is no darkness or evil at all. The question of judgment, the anger of God, the issue of hell, and the consequences of sin and all these other negative things never came up in the beginning. Only when Lucifer became Satan, and only when Eve and Adam were overtaken by temptation from Satan, did all dreadful things and all the anti-good come into being. The only root of all evils anywhere is nothing else but sin.

In fact, the Bible, through the lips of Jesus, says the reason why hell and punishment came into being: "Then shall he say also unto them on the left hand, Depart from me, ye cursed, into everlasting fire, prepared for the devil and his angels" (Matthew 25:41).

The Bible refers to Jesus Christ as the Creator Himself: "All things were made by him; and without him was not anything made that was made" (John 1:3).

"For by him were all things created, that are in heaven, and that are in earth, visible and invisible, whether they be thrones, or dominions, or principalities, or powers: all things were created by him, and for him: And he is before all things, and by him all things consist" (Colossians 1:16-17). Jesus is the full representative of God on earth, and He displayed the goodness of God in the absolute sense during His earthly ministry: "How God anointed Jesus of Nazareth with the Holy Ghost and with power: who went about doing good, for God was with Him" (Acts 10:38).

The summary of the entire ministry of Jesus Christ is, "And were beyond measure astonished, saying, He hath done all things well" (Mark 7:37).

God Is Love

God the Creator is absolute in whatever degree of attributes attached to him. In fact, He is referred to in Psalm 8:1 (KJV) in this way: "O Lord, our Lord, how excellent is thy name in all the earth! who hast set thy glory above the heavens." By this, it is confirmed that God is excellent in living out all His attributes beyond human comprehension. Whatever

He made originally was borne out of love. The glimpse of His love can be inferred from the following scriptures.

> Beloved, let us love one another: for love is of God; and every one that loveth is born of God, and knoweth God.
>
> He that loveth not knoweth not God; for God is love. And we have known and believed the love that God hath to us. God is love; and he that dwelleth in love dwelleth in God, and God in him.
>
> Herein is our love made perfect, that we may have boldness in the Day of Judgment: because as he is, so are we in this world. If a man say, I love God, and hateth his brother, he is a liar: for he that loveth not his brother whom he hath seen, how can he love God whom he hath not seen?
>
> And this commandment have we from him, that he who loveth God love his brother also. (1 John 4:7, 16–17, 20)

The apostle Paul was used of God to spell out the expectations of creatures of God (those who are children of God) in 1 Corinthians 13-1-7 (KJV).

> Though I speak with the tongues of men and of angels, and have not charity, I am become as sounding brass, or a tinkling cymbal.
>
> And though I have the gift of prophecy, and understand all mysteries, and all knowledge; and though I have all faith, so that I could remove mountains, and have not charity, I am nothing.
>
> And though I bestow all my goods to feed the poor, and though I give my body to be burned, and have not charity, it profiteth me nothing.

Charity suffereth long, and is kind; charity envieth not; charity vaunteth not itself, is not puffed up,

Doth not behave itself unseemly, seeketh not her own, is not easily provoked, thinketh no evil;

Rejoiceth not in iniquity, but rejoiceth in the truth;

Beareth all things, believeth all things, hopeth all things, endureth all things.

If the aforementioned characteristics are expected from mortal beings, one cannot imagine the level of God's love, from whom all such blessings flow to fill everyone. In light of this, it can easily be concluded that only lovely things could emanate from Him, for whom it's written, "Thou lovest righteousness, and hatest wickedness: therefore God, thy God, hath anointed thee with the oil of gladness above thy fellows" (Psalm 45:7).

God of Abundance

God is generous with everything He has, and hence everything He made comes in great abundance. Even man, though He started with just one, was designed to be fruitful and multiply and replenish the earth. He said of all other creatures, "And God said, let the waters bring forth abundantly the moving creature that hath life, and fowl that may fly above the earth in the open firmament of heaven ... And God blessed them, saying, be fruitful, and multiply, and fill the waters in the seas, and let fowl multiply in the earth" (Genesis 1:20, 22).

All the very good things that God created were to multiply abundantly, as they were in the original state.

There was abundance of fishes with
all types and variety of species.
There was abundance of birds with
all types and variety of species.

There was abundance of insects with
all types and variety of species.
There was abundance of animals with
all types and variety of species.
There was abundance of vegetables
with all variety of species.
There was abundance of sand.
There was abundance of rivers and oceans.
There were abundance of hills and mountains.
There were abundance of trees and fruits.

Little wonder that Jesus Christ promised all believers, "I am come That they might have life and that they might have it more abundantly" (John10:10).

Whatever God gives, He does abundantly to show His generosity and magnanimity. "Nevertheless he left not himself without witness, in that he did good, and gave us rain from heaven, and fruitful seasons, filling our hearts with food and gladness" (Acts 14:17).

The Psalmist says,

Thou visitest the earth, and waterest it: thou greatly enrichest it with the river of God, which is full of water: thou preparest them corn, when thou hast so provided for it.

Thou waterest the ridges thereof abundantly: thou settlest the furrows thereof: thou makest it soft with showers: thou blessest the springing thereof.

Thou crownest the year with thy goodness; and thy paths drop fatness.

They drop upon the pastures of the wilderness: and the little hills rejoice on every side.

The pastures are clothed with flocks; the valleys also are covered over with corn; they shout for joy, they also sing. (Psalm 65:9–13)

Jeremiah reveals the following in a powerful manner.

Therefore they shall come and sing in the height of Zion, and shall flow together to the goodness of the Lord, for wheat, and for wine, and for oil, and for the young of the flock and of the herd: and their soul shall be as a watered garden; and they shall not sorrow any more at all. Then shall the virgin rejoice in the dance, both young men and old together: for I will turn their mourning into joy, and will comfort them, and make them rejoice from their sorrow. And I will satiate the soul of the priests with fatness, and my people shall be satisfied with my goodness, saith the Lord. (Jeremiah 31:12–14)

God's abundance cannot be quantified by any means because all He needs to do is make them appear where there was none just by the thought of it or by the spoken word, as it was in the book of Genesis. He can bring water out of the rock. He can bring pools of rivers to emerge from the dry land. He can create things out of nothing. "As it is written, I have made thee a father of many nations,) before him whom he believed, even God, who quickeneth the dead, and calleth those things which be not as though they were" (Romans 4:17).

Abundance of life, abundance of provision in a godly way, and abundance of peace are the products of satisfaction. They produce the godly pleasures that God intended in creation. That was the very mind of God. It projects his goodness to all when all is good and all feel happy under the rule of a good God. Apostle Paul, at Philippians 4:19 (KJV), said, "But my God shall supply all your need according to his riches in glory by Christ Jesus." And Apostle John, the beloved, was speaking the mind of God when he proclaimed the original plan of God in 3 John

2:2 (KJV), "Beloved, I wish above all things that thou mayest prosper and be in health, even as thy soul prospereth."

Moreover, the confirmation of the intended pleasures of God for which He designed all things can only be summed up as follows: "The blessing of the Lord, it maketh rich, and he addeth no sorrow with it" (Proverbs 10:22).

This was real and factual in the original plan of God. How wonderful and befitting that it was meant to be so forever. How glorious it would have been if all things continued as it started in the Garden of Eden for all eternity. It would have been so perfectly proclaimed as it was in Luke 15:31–32, "And he said unto him, Son, thou art ever with me, and all that I have is thine. It was meet that we should make merry, and be glad."

Merriment in abundance in a godly sense, in the presence of the almighty God, in purity, and in righteous would have been a normal way of life. After all, the Earth is the Lord's, and the fullness thereof and His glory is supposed to cover everywhere. However, there is a period of pulse for the time being. It's only a pulse; the Lord's initial design and desires shall still come into a reality in the nearest future. It is a matter of time.

God of Beauty and Perfection

It is expected of a creative person to be a lover of beauty. God is no doubt a creator par excellence, and hence His love for things that are absolutely beautiful cannot be gainsaid. Everything created in their original form had his trade mark of 'very good'. Little wonder the Bible says in Ecclesiastes 3:11 (KJV), "He hath made everything beautiful in his time: also he hath set the world in their heart, so that no man can find out the work that God maketh from the beginning to the end."

This scripture of truth does not exclude anything made by God. In fact, the signature of God and His deeds were revealed by the declaration of all that witnessed the deeds of Jesus Christ when they said in Mark 7:37 (KJV), "And were beyond measure astonished, saying, He hath done all things well."

We do not expect less from a perfect God, a mighty God, an awesome God, a rich God, a resourceful God, an all-wise God who actually loves to exhibit His glory and delights in order to receive praises for His handiwork. Isaiah the prophet declares,

> In the year that king Uzziah died I saw also the Lord sitting upon a throne, high and lifted up, and his train filled the temple.
>
> Above it stood the seraphims: each one had six wings; with twain he covered his face, and with twain he covered his feet, and with twain he did fly.
>
> And one cried unto another, and said, Holy, holy, holy, is the LORD of hosts: the whole earth is full of his glory. (Isaiah 6:1–3)

God's works are so painstakingly executed that the standard of their beauty cannot be debated.

> Are not those flowers beautiful?
> Are not the seas and oceans beautiful?
> Are not those green grasses and shrubs beautiful?
> Are not the butterflies and vast
> number of insects beautiful?
> Are the sands by the seashore not beautiful?
> Are eagles, sparrows, nightingales, owls,
> and other birds not beautiful?
> Are tigers, zebras, lions, giraffes, elephants,
> and other species not beautiful?
> Are stars, the moon, sunshine, the sky,
> and the galaxies not beautiful?
> Are these uncountable trees and fruits not beautiful?
> Are these men and women, originally fearfully
> and wonderfully made, not beautiful?

How about the whales, The dolphins, The catfish, and myriads of sea creatures?

Is it beautiful when the wind blows gently to massage the bodies of all creatures?

You bet that all things great and small were made beautiful by the God who delights in beautiful things. It's part of the attribute of pleasures approved by God, the Creator.

There is no doubt the Garden of Eden, where He put Adam and Eve, was super beautiful. It was His original plan to replicate such by commanding that they be fruitful and multiply and replenish the earth. Everywhere was meant to be such beautiful. The Bible says, "God is not 'a respecter of persons'" (Acts 10:34). Therefore, what Adam and Eve enjoyed, He wanted all others to equally enjoy.

The description of the beauty of one angel, the Tabernacle in the wilderness during the trip of the Israelites from Egypt to the Promised Land, and the divine approval of the beautiful Temple in Jerusalem in the days of Solomon are testimonies of God's delight for beauty.

The Angel

Here is the description of Lucifer before he became Satan, or the devil. The colossal beauty of the angel alone is mind-boggling.

> Moreover the word of the LORD came unto me, saying,

> Son of man, take up a lamentation upon the king of Tyrus, and say unto him, Thus saith the Lord GOD; Thou sealest up the sum, full of wisdom, and perfect in beauty.

> Thou hast been in Eden the garden of God; every precious stone was thy covering, the sardius, topaz, and the diamond, the beryl, the onyx, and the jasper, the sapphire, the emerald, and the carbuncle, and gold: the workmanship of thy tabrets and of thy pipes was prepared in thee in the day that thou wast created.

Thou art the anointed cherub that covereth; and I have set thee so: thou wast upon the holy mountain of God; thou hast walked up and down in the midst of the stones of fire.

Thou wast perfect in thy ways from the day that thou wast created, till iniquity was found in thee._O covering cherub, from the midst of the stones of fire.

Thine heart was lifted up because of thy beauty, thou hast corrupted thy wisdom by reason of thy brightness: I will cast thee to the ground, I will lay thee before kings, that they may behold thee. (Ezekiel 28:11–17)

The Tabernacle

Even though this was to be erected in the wilderness, God did not compromise the standard of its beauty. In fact, He strictly commanded Moses *in Exodus 25:9, "According to all that I shew thee, after the pattern of the tabernacle, and the pattern of all the instruments thereof, even so shall ye make it."* Even those who were to work on the tabernacle were specially selected, talented, and spirit-filled workers. The pattern given to Moses and all the details in Exodus 25 shows God's admiration for perfection.

A glimpse of the beauty is described.

And thou shalt make a mercy seat of pure gold: two cubits and a half shall be the length thereof, and a cubit and a half the breadth thereof.

And thou shalt make two cherubims of gold, of beaten work shalt thou make them, in the two ends of the mercy seat.

And make one cherub on the one end, and the other cherub on the other end: even of the mercy seat shall ye make the cherubims on the two ends thereof.

And the cherubims shall stretch forth their wings on high, covering the mercy seat with their wings, and their faces shall look one to another; toward the mercy seat shall the faces of the cherubims be. (Exodus 25:17–20)

The Priests' Garments

It is also amazing how delightful God is with beauty and perfection that a special kind of beautiful garments had to be made for Aaron and his children to serve as high priests in the tabernacle.

And thou shalt speak unto all that are wise hearted, whom I have filled with the spirit of wisdom, that they may make Aaron's garments to consecrate him that he may minister unto me in the priest's office.

And these are the garments which they shall make; a breastplate, and an ephod, and a robe, and a broidered coat, a mitre, and a girdle: and they shall make holy garments for Aaron thy brother, and his sons, that he may minister unto me in the priest's office.

And they shall take gold, and blue, and purple, and scarlet, and fine linen.

And they shall make the ephod of gold, of blue, and of purple, of scarlet, and fine twined linen, with cunning work. (Exodus 28:3-6

Think about the elegance and meticulous attention to details! God stopped at nothing to pour his pleasure for excellence even in garments of his ministers.

And thou shalt set in it settings of stones, even four rows of stones: the first row shall be a sardius, a topaz, and a carbuncle: this shall be the first row.

And the second row shall be an emerald, a sapphire, and a diamond.

And the third row a ligure, an agate, and an amethyst.

And the fourth row a beryl, and an onyx, and a jasper: they shall be set in gold in their inclosings. (Exodus 28:17-20).

It is significant to note that the major reason for gorgeous garments of the priests was because they were to appear before God on the behalf of the people. That tells much about the pleasure of God in beauty, perfection and magnificence.

And Aaron shall bear the names of the children of Israel in the breastplate of judgment upon his heart, when he goeth in unto the holy place, for a memorial before the Lord continually.(Exodus 28:29).

And thou shalt embroider the coat of fine linen, and thou shalt make the mitre of fine linen, and thou shalt make the girdle of needlework.

And for Aaron's sons thou shalt make coats, and thou shalt make for them girdles, and bonnets shalt thou make for them, for glory and for beauty.

And thou shalt put them upon Aaron thy brother, and his sons with him; and shalt anoint them, and consecrate them, and sanctify them that they may minister unto me in the priest's office. (Exodus 28:–39-41).

You cannot read the above and not shout, "Oh, my world!" by reason of the high taste of the almighty God in respect to beauty and perfection. All things were so designed for His pleasure and were created. All these go to show the mind of God in respect to His original desires and intentions toward all His creatures.

God of Joy and Happiness

If there is anything that is absolutely pleasurable, it is experiencing joy within and all around you. There is no iota of doubt that God, the Creator of good things is a God of joy. If that be the case, why will He wish or ever desire anything that will make anything that came out of his joyful and good heart to experience sorrow, pain, anguish, sickness, afflictions, and hell? In the beginning of creation, everything was a bundle of joy and happiness. Everything was good to the body, good to the soul, good to the spirit, and in the atmosphere of a good environment. They were meant to bring joy and nothing harmful to all creatures. In fact, the Creator rejoiced over the works of His hands and fulfilled His own law from Matthew 22:39, "And the second is like unto it, Thou shalt love thy neighbour as thyself." And Matthew 7:12 states, "Therefore all things whatsoever ye would that men should do to you, do ye even so to them: for this is the law and the prophets."

And His perfect definition of love is spelled out that it "thinketh no evil" (1 Corinthians 13:5). That being the case, the fact is that God constantly experiences joy without any sorrow whatsoever: "Thou wilt shew me the path of life: in thy presence is fulness of joy; at thy right hand there are pleasures for evermore" (Psalm 16:11). And of course, Romans 14:17 (KJV) states, "For the kingdom of God is not meat and drink; but righteousness, and peace, and joy in the Holy Ghost." It was never His plan or agenda to separate Himself from His creatures, and hence the joy from Him was originally supposed to be perpetually shared before sin came in. The manifestations in His domain and kingdom are perpetually characterized by righteousness and joy. No wonder Jesus Christ urged the believers in John 16:24 (KJV), "Hitherto have ye asked nothing in my name: ask, and ye shall receive, that your joy may be full." Apostle Paul also followed suit, admonishing in Philippians 4:4, "Rejoice in the Lord always: and again I say, Rejoice."

Suffice it to state that God who commands His creatures to rejoice: "Rejoice with them that do rejoice" (Romans 12:15) cannot be the source of sorrow and lamentations. In attestation to the fact that He desires joy and is pleasured by the joy of all His creation, Christ's ministry was centered on restoring the original plan of God: "Surely he hath borne our griefs, and carried our sorrows: yet we did esteem him stricken, smitten of God, and afflicted" (Isaiah 53:4).

The New Testament confirms that in Luke 4:18–19 (KJV), "The Spirit of the Lord is upon me, because he hath anointed me to preach the gospel to the poor; he hath sent me to heal the brokenhearted, to preach deliverance to the captives, and recovering of sight to the blind, to set at liberty them that are bruised."

Apostle Peter summarized the entire ministry of the Son of God in Acts 10:38, "How God anointed Jesus of Nazareth with the Holy Ghost and with power: who went about doing good, and healing all that were oppressed of the devil; for God was with him." The apostles continued ministrations and were confirmed from heaven with miracles, signs, and wonders.

> Then Philip went down to the city of Samaria, and preached Christ unto them. And the people with one accord gave heed unto those things which Philip spake, hearing and seeing the miracles which he did.
>
> For unclean spirits, crying with loud voice, came out of many that were possessed with them: and many taken with palsies, and that were lame, were healed.
>
> And there was great joy in that city. (Acts 8:5–6)

The reasons for God's support that produced healings, miracles, salvation, signs, and wonders was primarily to bring joy to everyone and praises and adoration to the source of those wonders. Actually, all the talk on the ministration of the laws, the prophets, the coming of Jesus Christ to the earth, and the proclamation of the good news is centered on full restitution of the original plan of God to eventually culminate in all things being created for His pleasures, and that will become reality at the end of age. This was certainly the original plan and desire of God.

Come to think of it, what was the shout of the host of angels at the birth of Jesus Christ, the Savior and Redeemer, about?

And there were in the same country shepherds abiding in the field, keeping watch over their flock by night. And, lo, the angel of the Lord came upon them, and the glory of the Lord shone round about them: and they were sore afraid. And the angel said unto them, Fear not: for, behold, I bring you good tidings of great joy, which shall be to all people. For unto you is born this day in the city of David a Savior, which is Christ the Lord. (Luke 2:8–11)

After the revelation from the angels of God about the good news (glad tidings, the Gospel), what followed thereafter was to express the utmost desire of God to all creatures. "And suddenly there was with the angel a multitude of the heavenly host praising God, and saying, Glory to God in the highest, and on earth peace, good will toward men."(Luke 2:13-14)

It has been His plan to make all of His creatures to enjoy the rivers of His goodly and godly pleasures. Now He makes another final push to doing so by sending His only begotten Son to the world. What is the importance of good news to anyone, by the way?

As cold waters to a thirsty soul, so is good news from a far country. (Proverbs 25:25)

How beautiful upon the mountains are the feet of him that bringeth good tidings, that publisheth peace; that bringeth good tidings of good that publisheth salvation; that saith unto Zion, Thy God reigneth! (Isaiah 52:7)

The very desire of the merciful Creator is to satisfy all His creatures with His good pleasures. The reason for this is that scriptures and the original plan of God might be fulfilled.

To trust in the living God, who giveth us richly all things to enjoy. (1 Timothy 6:17)

> That all creatures might rejoice before thee according to the joy in harvest, and as men rejoice when they divide the spoil. (Isaiah 9:3)

Isn't God a God of joy and happiness, and the joy and happiness of His creatures are pleasing to Him? Little wonder the word of God says in *1 Thessalonians* 5:16 (KJV), "Rejoice evermore." He projects it further in Isaiah 51:11 (KJV), "Therefore the redeemed of the Lord shall return, and come with singing unto Zion; and everlasting joy shall be upon their head: they shall obtain gladness and joy; and sorrow and mourning shall flee away."

God of Pleasures

God, the Creator of good things, is doubtless the God of pleasures. Of course this has nothing to do with ungodly or perverse ones. He never designed such in any of His creatures or planned that for them. He wanted all to be at the boundaries of all the good and lovely pleasures in all aspects and to have them in abundance too. It should be buttressed again and again that all the thoughts of God are perfectly good, and in Him there is no evil, darkness, or wickedness at all. If therefore all things were created for His pleasure, and they all exist for His pleasure, then God must be a God of pleasures.

It pleasures God that everything is perfect: "The Lord will perfect that which concerneth me" (Psalm 138:8).

It pleasures God that everyone is happy and joyful: "Even them will I bring to my holy mountain, and make them joyful in my house of prayer" (Isaiah 56:7 KJV).

It pleasures God that all is well with all things He created: "And were beyond measure astonished, saying, He hath done all things well" (Mark 7:37 KJV).

It pleasures God that none lacks any good thing: "For the Lord God is a sun and shield: the Lord will give grace and glory: no good thing will he withhold from them that walk uprightly" (Psalm 84:11).

It pleasures God that no one is barren: "There shall nothing cast their young, nor be barren" (Exodus 23:26).

It pleasures God that all needs are supplied to all His creatures: "These wait all upon thee; that thou mayest give them their meat in due season" (Psalms 104:27).

It pleasures God to rejoice and merry:

> And the third day there was a marriage in Cana of Galilee; and the mother of Jesus was there:

> And both Jesus was called, and his disciples, to the marriage.

> And when they wanted wine, the mother of Jesus saith unto him, they have no wine.

> Jesus saith unto her, Woman, what have I to do with thee? mine hour is not yet come.

> His mother saith unto the servants, Whatsoever he saith unto you, do it.

> And there were set there six water pots of stone, after the manner of the purifying of the Jews, containing two or three firkins apiece.

> Jesus saith unto them, Fill the water pots with water. And they filled them up to the brim.

> And he saith unto them, Draw out now, and bear unto the governor of the feast. And they bare it.

> When the ruler of the feast had tasted the water that was made wine, and knew not whence it was: (but the servants which drew the water knew ;) the governor of the feast called the bridegroom,

> And saith unto him, every man at the beginning doth set forth good wine; and when men have well drunk,

then that which is worse: but thou hast kept the good wine until now. (John 2:1–10)

Jesus Christ narrated and approved another story again where this was well illustrated in Luke 15:32, "It was meet that we should make merry, and be glad: for this thy brother was dead, and is alive again; and was lost, and is found."

It pleasures God to have good success: "This book of the law shall not depart out of thy mouth; but thou shalt meditate therein day and night, that thou mayest observe to do according to all that is written therein: for then thou shalt make thy way prosperous, and then thou shalt have good success" (Joshua 1:8).

It pleasures God that all is comforted on every side: "Thou shalt increase my greatness, and comfort me on every side. I will also praise thee with the psaltery, even thy truth, O my God: unto thee will I sing with the harp, O thou Holy One of Israel" (Psalm 71:21–23 KJV).

It pleasures God that all live and not die: "Have I any pleasure at all that the wicked should die? saith the Lord God: and not that he should return from his ways, and live?" (Ezekiel 18:23 KJV).

It pleasures God that all things are made possible for all: "And Jesus said unto them, Because of your unbelief: for verily I say unto you, If ye have faith as a grain of mustard seed, ye shall say unto this mountain, Remove hence to yonder place; and it shall remove; and nothing shall be impossible unto you" (Matthew 17:20).

It pleasures God that goodness and mercies follow everyone forever: "Surely goodness and mercy shall follow me all the days of my life: and I will dwell in the house of the Lord forever" (Psalm 23:6 KJV).

It pleasures God to prosper in all areas of endeavors: "Beloved, I wish above all things that thou mayest prosper and be in health, even as thy soul prospereth." (3 John 1:2 KJV)

But thou shalt remember the LORD thy God: for it is he that giveth thee power to get wealth. (Deuteronomy 8:18)

And he shall be like a tree planted by the rivers of water, that bringeth forth his fruit in his season; his leaf also shall not wither; and whatsoever he doeth shall prosper. (Psalm 1:3 KJV)

It pleasures God to grant grace to all: "For the grace of God that bringeth salvation hath appeared to all men" (Titus 2:11 KJV).

It pleasures God to fellowship with all:"That they should seek the Lord, if haply they might feel after him, and find him, though he be not far from every one of us" (Acts 17:27).

It pleasures God to love all:

For there is no respect of persons with God." (Romans 2:11 KJV)

For God so loved the world, that he gave his only begotten Son, that whosoever believeth in him should not perish, but have everlasting life. (John 3:16 KJV)

It pleasures God to have everyone be like Him: "And God said, Let us make man in our image, after our likeness" (Genesis 1:26 KJV).

It pleasures God to be served in gladness and singing: "Serve the LORD with gladness: come before his presence with singing" (Psalms 100:2).

It pleasures God to have praises: "But thou art holy, O thou that inhabitest the praises of Israel" (Psalm 22:3 KJV).

It pleasures God to protect everyone:

I will never leave thee nor forsake thee. (Hebrews 13:5)

For I, saith the LORD, will be unto her a wall of fire round about, and will be the glory in the midst of her. (Zechariah 2:5)

God is pleasured by worship: "And all the angels stood round about the throne, and about the elders and the four beasts, and fell before the throne on their faces, and worshipped God, Saying, Amen: Blessing, and glory, and wisdom, and thanksgiving, and honour, and power, and might, be unto our God for ever and ever. Amen" (Revelation 7:11–12).

It pleasures God to endow gifts unto everyone: "Every good gift and every perfect gift is from above, and cometh down from the Father of lights, with whom is no variableness, neither shadow of turning" (James 1:17).

All these are testimonies to the original delight of God in all His creatures—not just for a temporary period of time but on a permanent and forever basis. All these and many more were designed to be the pleasures of all things as a daily experience. It was sin that marred all these, which had its root in Satan, temptation, the fall, God's wrath, and eviction from the Garden of Eden.

> Wherefore, as by one man sin entered into the world, and death by sin; and so death passed upon all men, for that all have sinned:
>
> For until the law sin was in the world: but sin is not imputed when there is no law.
>
> Nevertheless death reigned from Adam to Moses, even over them that had not sinned after the similitude of Adam's transgression, who is the figure of him that was to come." (Romans 5:12–14 KJV)
>
> "For all have sinned, and come short of the glory of God"(Romans 3:23).
>
> However all of God's pleasures cannot be fully realized any longer in this present world hence God has to make a way to fulfil this permanently in the nearest future.

Five

---- ✍ ----

REASONS FOR CHRIST

The major reasons why Christ Jesus came to this world are clearly stated. "He that committeth sin is of the devil; for the devil sinneth from the beginning. For this purpose the Son of God was manifested, that he might destroy the works of the devil" (1 John 3:8).

It is a confirmed fact of the scriptures that the very beginning of any problem in heaven or earth was a result of sin (rebellion or disobedience to God, the almighty Creator of the heavens and the earth). Originally, all was well with everything God created, until sin came in. This brought about God's displeasures against Satan and His angels, as well as Adam and Eve, affecting their environment. The original blessings of the Creator turned to curses.

The manifestation of Jesus Christ on Earth was to deal with the root of the problem, which is sin, and if sin was to be dealt with, the consequences of sin had to be dealt with as well.

The devil, who is said to be the originator of sin ("He that committeth sin is of the devil; for the devil sinneth from the beginning"1John 3:8a), was Lucifer. He was created a perfect angel, without sin at the beginning. He was the tempter who lured Eve and Adam to sin against God, just as he sinned in heaven, thereby causing a change to the hitherto wonderful and God-given things. Corruption came into man, affecting everything around him. Hence, "all have sinned and come short of the glory of God." (Romans 3:23).Everything now came under the wrath of God except heaven, because the originator of sin, Satan and his angels, were driven out of it. "Therefore rejoice, ye heavens, and ye that dwell in them. Woe to the inhabiters of the earth and of the sea! For the devil is come down unto you, having great wrath, because he knoweth that he hath but a short time" (Revelation 12:12)

Man was given the dominion over the earth, and it has been lost to Satan through disobedience. The means through which God decided to redeem everything back to the original state was through the death and resurrection of Jesus Christ, His only begotten Son.

> Wherefore, as by one man sin entered into the world, and death by sin; and so death passed upon all men, for that all have sinned:

> (For until the law sin was in the world: but sin is not imputed when there is no law.

> Nevertheless death reigned from Adam to Moses, even over them that had not sinned after the similitude of Adam's transgression, who is the figure of him that was to come.

> But not as the offence, so also is the free gift. For if through the offence of one many be dead, much more the grace of God, and the gift by grace, which is by one man, Jesus Christ, hath abounded unto many.

> And not as it was by one that sinned, so is the gift: for the judgment was by one to condemnation, but the free gift is of many offences unto justification.

> For if by one man's offence death reigned by one; much more they which receive abundance of grace and of the gift of righteousness shall reign in life by one, Jesus Christ.)

> Therefore as by the offence of one judgment came upon all men to condemnation; even so by the righteousness

of one the free gift came upon all men unto justification of life.

For as by one man's disobedience many were made sinners, so by the obedience of one shall many be made righteous.

Moreover the law entered, that the offence might abound. But where sin abounded, grace did much more abound:

That as sin hath reigned unto death, even so might grace reign through righteousness unto eternal life by Jesus Christ our Lord. (Romans 5:12–21)

Christ came to reconcile man back with God. The relationship, which was hitherto estranged, was now being restored so all creatures might be redeemed.

But now in Christ Jesus ye who sometimes were far off are made nigh by the blood of Christ.

For he is our peace, who hath made both one, and hath broken down the middle wall of partition between us;

Having abolished in his flesh the enmity, even the law of commandments contained in ordinances; for to make in himself of twain one new man, so making peace;

And that he might reconcile both unto God in one body by the cross, having slain the enmity thereby:

And came and preached peace to you which were afar off, and to them that were nigh.

For through him we both have access by one Spirit unto the Father.

Now therefore ye are no more strangers and foreigners, but fellow citizens with the saints, and of the household of God. (Ephesians 2:13–19)

The scriptures confirm the privileges of reconciliation of man with God through repentance from sins and believing in Jesus Christ

For God so loved the world, that he gave his only begotten Son, that whosoever believeth in him should not perish, but have everlasting life.

For God sent not his Son into the world to condemn the world; but that the world through him might be saved.

He that believeth on him is not condemned: but he that believeth not is condemned already, because he hath not believed in the name of the only begotten Son of God. (John 3:16–18)

The end result of faith in Christ is redemption of humankind and salvation to the lost man at the garden.

But God, who is rich in mercy, for his great love wherewith he loved us, Even when we were dead in sins, hath quickened us together with Christ, (by grace ye are saved;)

And hath raised us up together, and made us sit together in heavenly places in Christ Jesus:

That in the ages to come he might shew the exceeding riches of his grace in his kindness toward us through Christ Jesus.

For by grace are ye saved through faith; and that not of yourselves: it is the gift of God?

Not of works, lest any man should boast. (Ephesians 2:4–9)

There is now the promise of living eternally in fellowship with God and forever enjoying the pleasures and not the displeasures or the wrath of God, which began at the Garden of Eden. It sounds more like the very desires and aspirations of God from the beginning of creation. That is to say, at the end of all things, the good gestures of the almighty and perfect Creator will eventually come into a reality, but only for the believers in Christ Jesus. Others who refuse the gift of God for pardon and redemption through Jesus Christ will face the wrath and judgment of God by everlasting punishment in hellfire: "But the fearful, and unbelieving, and the abominable, and murderers, and whoremongers, and sorcerers, and idolaters, and all liars, shall have their part in the lake which burneth with fire and brimstone: which is the second death" (Revelation 21:8).

There is also the promise of restitution of all things to become as pleasurable as God will have it at the close of all things.

> For I reckon that the sufferings of this present time are not worthy to be compared with the glory which shall be revealed in us.

> For the earnest expectation of the creature waiteth for the manifestation of the sons of God.

> For the creature was made subject to vanity, not willingly, but by reason of him who hath subjected the same in hope,

> Because the creature itself also shall be delivered from the bondage of corruption into the glorious liberty of the children of God.

> For we know that the whole creation groaneth and travaileth in pain together until now.

> And not only they, but ourselves also, which have the firstfruits of the Spirit, even we ourselves groan

within ourselves, waiting for the adoption, to wit, the redemption of our body. (Romans 8:18–23)

Looking back at the Garden of Eden, all the events before the fall of man, and the aftermath, until the coming of Christ and the promised eternal life, there are many questions with respect to what would have been. However, it is clear that God originally had all things set as very good, and all things were created for His pleasures and were meant to remain so as long as everything cooperated with the Creator. It is so clear that at the end of all things, God will still have His desire to fulfill the original goal according to His promise: "And he that sat upon the throne said, Behold, I make all things new. And he said unto me, Write: for these words are true and faithful. And he said unto me, it is done. I am Alpha and Omega, the beginning and the end" (Revelation 21:5–6). In Isaiah 46:9–13, God declares,

Remember the former things of old: for I am God, and there is none else; I am God, and there is none like me, Declaring the end from the beginning, and from ancient times the things that are not yet done, saying, My counsel shall stand, and I will do all my pleasure:

Calling a ravenous bird from the east, the man that executeth my counsel from a far country: yea, I have spoken it, I will also bring it to pass; I have purposed it, I will also do it. Hearken unto me, ye stouthearted that are far from righteousness:

I bring near my righteousness; it shall not be far off, and my salvation shall not tarry: and I will place salvation in Zion for Israel my glory.

Six

THE MILLENNIUM: MINI ULTIMATE PLEASURES OF GOD

We should be reminded that this book is not about eschatological study of events but rather a peek into a few aspects as to the pleasures of God with respect to having everything in place for the maximum benefit and enjoyment for all His creatures. It is meant to show that from the very beginning, when the almighty Creator purposed in His mind to bring into being creatures, He was all out for the best.

> His desire was never to kill them.
> His desire was never to afflict them.
> His desire was never to oppress them.
> His desire was never to mistreat them.
> His desire was never to disorganize them.
> His desire was never to maltreat them.
> His desire was never to confuse them.
> His desire was never to ignore them.
> His desire was never to ridicule them.
> His desire was never to deny them of good things.
> His desire was never to make them sorrowful.
> His desire was never to sadden them.
> His desire was never to burden or shackle them.
> His desire was never to send them to hell.

He never planned to wield His power in a rough way against His creatures. He is a good God who set out to have the best for all His creatures and be responsible to each and every one of them without prejudice or favoritism. Hence the Psalmist says,

> But let the righteous be glad; let them rejoice before God: yea, let them exceedingly rejoice. Sing unto God, sing praises to his name: extol him that rideth upon the heavens by his name Jah, and rejoice before him. Thou, O God, didst send a plentiful rain, whereby thou didst confirm thine inheritance, when it was weary. Thy congregation hath dwelt therein: thou, O God, hast prepared of thy goodness for the poor. Blessed be the Lord, who daily loadeth us with benefits, even the God of our salvation. Selah. (Psalm 68:3–19)

Apostle Paul also wrote by the Spirit of God in 2 Corinthians 9:8 (KJV), "And God is able to make all grace abound toward you; that ye, always having all sufficiency in all things, may abound to every good work."

Therefore, the millennial reign of Christ on Earth is what the Bible records in prophecy to be a literal one thousand years of Christ's rule as King on Earth.

> And I saw an angel come down from heaven, having the key of the bottomless pit and a great chain in his hand. And he laid hold on the dragon, that old serpent, which is the Devil, and Satan, and bound him a thousand years,
>
> And cast him into the bottomless pit, and shut him up, and set a seal upon him, that he should deceive the nations no more, till the thousand years should be fulfilled: and after that he must be loosed a little season.
>
> And I saw thrones, and they sat upon them, and judgment was given unto them: and I saw the souls of

them that were beheaded for the witness of Jesus, and for the word of God, and which had not worshipped the beast, neither his image, neither had received his mark upon their foreheads, or in their hands; and they lived and reigned with Christ a thousand years.

But the rest of the dead lived not again until the thousand years were finished. This is the first resurrection.

Blessed and holy is he that hath part in the first resurrection: on such the second death hath no power, but they shall be priests of God and of Christ, and shall reign with him a thousand years.

And when the thousand years are expired, Satan shall be loosed out of his prison. (Revelation 20:1–7)

The importance and the significance of this period are the wonderful things that will characterize the entire thousand years is significant to the desires of God and His pleasures for His creatures.

1. A world without Satan or any satanic influence at all will be the order of the entire period, for the Bible says Satan, the tempter and the source of all the woes that started in the Garden of Eden, will be imprisoned for one thousand years. Let's remember that at the inception of the Garden of Eden, Satan was not involved. It goes without saying that all the activities of Satan will be suspended across the world at time of the millennium. Jesus Christ will be in absolute control of all things with His almighty power.

2. There will be an international kingdom of unparalleled spirituality, and people will be unified to worship the only true God.

3. The purposes of God for the whole earth will be in full manifestation—a theocratic government.

4. Only the laws of the true God will be in force throughout this long period of time without rivals.

5. The kingdom of this world will become the kingdom of God and Jesus Christ.

6. The earthly kingdom of Christ will be glorious and majestic.

7. There will be a spread of divine mercy across the world.

8. Righteousness will cover the whole world.

9. There will be goodness across the board—a reminder of the very good and pleasant environment in the Garden of Eden.

10. Truth will be the bedrock of all activities.

11. Christ the ruler will display His divine, omnipotent, and omniscient prowess.

12. Worldly and Satan-influenced setups will be overthrown at the emergence of Christ's divine rule.

13. There shall be elimination of sin and all forms of unrighteousness.

14. There shall be uninterrupted peace in all spheres of life because the Prince of Peace will be ruling and reigning.

15. Every knee will bow to the only true God, and every tongue will swear allegiance to Him.

16. Jesus, the King, will sit on David's throne in Jerusalem, whose reign over Israel and who's worldwide kingdom will never end.

17. It will be a kingdom in which nature will be altered and curses will be removed.

18. There will be harmony between animals and human beings with no attacks of any sort. Hence, it will be a government without fears.

19. There will be sound health and an economic boom.

20. There shall be no wars between nations throughout the thousand years of Christ's reign on earth.

21. There will be abundance for all creatures.

22. There shall be complete freedom from all forms of oppression.

Judging from the overflow of goodness, peace, purity, and prosperity during the thousand years of Christ's rule on Earth, it can safely be said that it will perfectly align with the desires of God at the beginning, when creation began before sin marred the agenda. This period will definitely witness nothing but the pleasures of God, which is characteristic of His goodwill toward all His creatures. This goes to show that indeed, creation was designed for pleasures. After the thousand years, there will be a period of termination because the Bible says Satan will be released again, resulting in diverse sinfulness, temptations, and chaos in the world again. "And when the thousand years are expired, Satan shall be loosed out of his prison" (Revelation 20:7).

The fact that Satan will be released for a short time after the thousand years of Christ's rule is the very reason for referring to the millennium period as a period of the mini ultimate pleasures of God.

Seven

THE UTMOST PLEASURES OF GOD

Ultimately, God must have His way.

Ultimately, He must fulfill His pleasures.

Ultimately, He must display to all His creature all His goodness, all His lovingkindness, all His glory, all of His ingenuity, all His capabilities, and all His wisdom, knowledge, and understanding. He must eventually show all His purity, all His powers, all His riches, and all of His mercies, but this will come to full manifestation at the commencement of a new heaven and a new Earth.

> And I saw a new heaven and a new earth: for the first heaven and the first earth were passed away; and there was no more sea.

> And I John saw the holy city, New Jerusalem, coming down from God out of heaven, prepared as a bride adorned for her husband.

> And I heard a great voice out of heaven saying, Behold, the tabernacle of God is with men, and he will dwell with them, and they shall be his people, and God himself

shall be with them, and be their God. (Revelation 21:1–5)

This will be the ultimate fulfillment of all the pleasures of God to all creatures. And the good news is that it will not be like the Garden of Eden that lasted for just a period of time. Neither will it be like the thousand years of Christ's reign on Earth. This will be forever and without an end, amen.

Apostle Peter said,

But the heavens and the earth, which are now, by the same word are kept in store, reserved unto fire against the Day of Judgment and perdition of ungodly men.

But, beloved, be not ignorant of this one thing, that one day is with the Lord as a thousand years, and a thousand years as one day.

The Lord is not slack concerning his promise, as some men count slackness; but is longsuffering to us-ward, not willing that any should perish, but that all should come to repentance. But the day of the Lord will come as a thief in the night; in the heavens shall pass away with a great noise, and the elements shall melt with fervent heat, the earth also and the works that are therein shall be burned up.

Seeing then that all these things shall be dissolved, what manner of persons ought ye to be in all holy conversation and godliness, looking for and hasting unto the coming of the day of God, wherein the heavens being on fire shall be dissolved, and the elements shall melt with fervent heat? Nevertheless we, according to his promise, look for new heavens and a new earth, wherein dwelleth righteousness. (2 Peter 3:7–13)

Jesus Christ, the savior of the world, also emphasized to His followers in John 14:1–3 (KJV), "Let not your heart be troubled: ye believe in

God, believe also in me. In my Father's house are many mansions: if it were not so, I would have told you. I go to prepare a place for you. And if I go and prepare a place for you, I will come again, and receive you unto myself; that where I am, there ye may be also."

Apostle Paul referenced this ultimate desire of God in Hebrews 11:13–16.

> These all died in faith, not having received the promises, but having seen them afar off, and were persuaded of them, and embraced them, and confessed that they were strangers and pilgrims on the earth.
>
> For they that say such things declare plainly that they seek a country.
>
> And truly, if they had been mindful of that country from whence they came out, they might have had opportunity to have returned.
>
> But now they desire a better country, that is, an heavenly: wherefore God is not ashamed to be called their God: for he hath prepared for them a city.

Jesus Christ Himself nailed the utmost desire of God in John 3:16 (KJV), "For God so loved the world, that he gave his only begotten Son, that whosoever believeth in him should not perish, but have everlasting life."

Everlasting life is life in the most abundant way possible in the very presence of God, the angels of God, and all those who take the advantage of the greatest opportunity of a lifetime by repenting of their sins, forsaking their sins, and believing in the Lord Jesus Christ as their personal Lord and Savior.

Let's have a glimpse of the ultimate pleasures of God masterfully designed in the new heaven and new Earth.

Apostle Paul captured this in such a magnificent way when he was inspired by the Spirit of God in 1 Corinthians 2:9 (KJV), "But as it is written, Eye hath not seen, nor ear heard, neither have entered into the heart of man, the things which God hath prepared for them that love him."

Nothing could be more profound and highly motivating than this description in respect to the ultimate pleasures of God to all His creatures. Critical analysis of this powerful statement for those who desire to enjoy this everlasting provision of God in heaven will reveal some outstanding facts. This will also motivate those who have yet to decide where to spend eternity to make up their minds while the opportunity is available.

What has eyes not seen since the creation of things? Whoa! By this, the apostle was referring to great things, wonderful things, enjoyable things, and pleasurable things. What then? Where? When? Till the close of the present world.

In the Garden of Eden, eyes had seen a lot in the form of beauty, perfection of the state of all things, fellowship with God, bliss between Adam and Eve while it lasted, and all other wonders. But the apostle says those were still little compared to the ultimate pleasures of God in heaven.

How about all other glamorous and wonderful things in various earthly kingdoms and empires, including that of Israel in the good old days? The man of God says no matter what people had seen in the best of the kingdoms of this world—riches, happiness, achievements, gold and silver, mansions or palaces, amusement and laughter, joy, peace, ecstatic events, holidays, honeymoons, fellowships, love, fun, unity, fantasies, spirituality, memorable days and years, turning points, miracles, signs and wonders, glories, exaltations and ovations, outstanding successes, all that money could buy, all that fame could amass, all privileges and advantages, all opportunities in the history of humankind put together—they can by no means match up to what God is preparing for the inhabitants of heaven.

In other words, the ultimate blessings, joy, and pleasures ever experienced here on Earth is nothing compared to all that God has in store for believers in Christ in heaven above.

The apostle did not stop in only what is visible in this world but goes deeper by saying that ears have not heard. This is no doubt mind-boggling! What have ears not heard?

About glories of kings and princes?

About riches and honors?

About power and extravagant lives of multibillionaires?

About amazing technologies and wisdom?

About elegance, pomp, and pageantry?

About love and affections?

About excellences or glories?

About riches and abundance?

About decencies and desires?

About architectural designs?

Name them. The man of God says whatever anyone has heard about, even about heaven, they are still not enough in comparison with the actual reality of the package of God in heaven for all His creatures.

The last part of this phrase, "or entered into the heart of man," is almost insane in the real sense of the word. This means that the glorious things God has prepared to lavish on all that will eventually be in heaven cannot be conceived by the imaginations of the most genius of all men, no matter how hard they try. Simply put, it's not possible for any man ever created to grasp fully all the stuff, the unimaginable blessings that will be lavished on all those who will enter into heaven to richly enjoy. Surely it is only in heaven that there will be the confirmation of the scriptures in Psalm 16:11 (KJV), "Thou wilt shew me the path of life: in thy presence is fullness of joy; at thy right hand there are pleasures for evermore."

Heaven, the abode of God, the almighty Creator, and the angels, is described moderately by the revelation according to Apostle John. What, then, are the pleasures of God designed for regarding all who will end up there to richly bask in them?

Heaven is said to be the most beautiful place beyond the description of any human imagination. According to the revelation shown unto Apostle John in Revelation 21:10–11, "And he carried me away in the spirit to a great and high mountain, and shewed me that great city, the holy Jerusalem, descending out of heaven from God, having the glory of God: and her light was like unto a stone most precious, even like a jasper stone, clear as crystal; 'Having the glory of God.'" The glory of

God cannot be described fully by a mortal man. That alone in heaven is worth all it takes to get there. Just to see the glory of God that Moses craved for in Exodus 33:18, "And he said, I beseech thee, shew me thy glory." Or that of Isaiah 6:1–4 (KJV):

> In the year that king Uzziah died I saw also the Lord sitting upon a throne, high and lifted up, and his train filled the temple. Above it stood the seraphims: each one had six wings; with twain he covered his face, and with twain he covered his feet, and with twain he did fly. And one cried unto another, and said, Holy, holy, holy, is the Lord of hosts: the whole earth is full of his glory. And the posts of the door moved at the voice of him that cried, and the house was filled with smoke.

The prophet had a glimpse of God's glory and was amazed. The experience of the three disciples on the month of transfiguration made Apostle Peter cry out in awe and wonders.

> And it came to pass about an eight days after these sayings, he took Peter and John and James, and went up into a mountain to pray.

> And as he prayed, the fashion of his countenance was altered, and his raiment was white and glistering. And, behold, there talked with him two men, which were Moses and Elias: Who appeared in glory, and spake of his decease which he should accomplish at Jerusalem. But Peter and they that were with him were heavy with sleep: and when they were awake, they saw his glory, and the two men that stood with him.

> And it came to pass, as they departed from him, Peter said unto Jesus, Master, it is good for us to be here: and let us make three tabernacles; one for thee, and one for Moses, and one for Elias: not knowing what he said. (Luke 9; 26–33 KJV)

Imagine seeing the most awesomely radiant and beautiful object that takes away all your breath! "Her light was like unto a stone most precious, even like a jasper stone, clear as crystal" (Revelation 21:11). Imagine experiencing the loveliest things that stay with you forever without wearing away! Imagine an inner feeling of something you cannot really explain so awesomely satisfying beyond your widest imaginations! Imagine experiencing overflow of unstoppable waves of love, lovingkindness, mercies, goodness, holy ecstasy beyond explanations altogether at the same time! Imagine having the brightness of billions of the brightness of the sun and stars altogether and without any hurting effects, but the beauty and brightness of them is so much so that there is not a speck of darkness anywhere!

> And the city had no need of the sun, neither of the moon, to shine in it: for the glory of God did lighten it, and the Lamb is the light thereof. And I saw no temple therein: for the Lord God Almighty and the Lamb are the temple of it. (Revelation 21:22–23)

Imagine having your utmost desires met billion times over and the met desires stay on forever without having any desire for greater or higher for all eternity! Imagine having all your being overtaken by unexplainable highest joy forever and ever and you wish for nothing greater or higher or deeper!

All these will still not be close to any percentage with respect to experiencing the glory of God in heaven. In short, the glory of God can be said to be in a lame man's human language perpetual, limitless experience of the best of all things with all the senses. The greatest desire of Christ from God the Father is that all believers should witness and experience the most spectacular thing in heaven: His glory.

John 17:24 states, "Father, I will that they also, whom thou hast given me, be with me where I am; that they may behold my glory, which thou hast given me: for thou lovedst me before the foundation of the world." If that singular request is weighty beyond other things in the heart of Jesus with respect to the splendor of the glory of God, then it must be counted as the utmost of all pleasures.

Other amazingly gorgeous things are painted and revealed in the revelation of heaven to Apostle John: "And the building of the wall of it was of jasper: and the city was pure gold, like unto clear glass." (Revelation 21:18)

The costliest material on earth is pure gold. Having a whole city completely built with the purest heavenly gold, not from the universe but with material directly from the almighty God Himself, whose work is perfect, beats one's imaginations. What pleasure will that be to look upon the entirety of heaven built with nothing but the purest of gold that never fades away forever and ever? One significant thing to also take notice of is that joyful feelings and that of admiration never wavers in heaven. Everything is constant in a sense that you never wish for less or more once in there. Everyone is in a perfect state just like God, and everything else is in a perfect state. This is incomparable with anything else.

Also take a deep breath and take up your thinking cap as we view the following along with Apostle John.

> And the foundations of the wall of the city were garnished with all manner of precious stones. The first foundation was jasper; the second, sapphire; the third, a chalcedony; the fourth, an emerald; The fifth, sardonyx; the sixth, sardius; the seventh, chrysolyte; the eighth, beryl; the ninth, a topaz; the tenth, a chrysoprasus; the eleventh, a jacinth; the twelfth, an amethyst. (Revelation 21:19–20)

Is there any point trying to describe each of these twelve materials one after another? For now, the best expression is *amazing*. Even if the types of these heavenly materials are found anywhere in the universe, you can be sure that they are subject to decay and fading in beauty and strength. But that of heaven, specially made for the foundation of the everlasting city of God, is most precious beyond comprehension and solid to last for all eternity. The architectural design of heaven attracts so much splendor that one cannot but agree that it was designed for pleasures to live in and to look upon. All that is in this heavenly city will never need modifications or modernization after billions of years because the project is at the best from the God, whose name is Alpha and Omega and whose works are perfect.

It was a deliberate thing to jump the queue by not following a kind of due order in the description of heaven. Due to the glory of God, the foundations and the walls of pure gold are too exciting to the heart that entering through the gate was left out.

Nevertheless, because everything around and within are too good to leave out, let's have a glimpse of the gates into the city, which are twelve in number. "And the twelve gates were twelve pearls: every several gate was of one pearl: and the street of the city was pure gold, as it were transparent glass" (Revelation 21:21). For the highly privileged individual who will be allowed to come through the gates and eventually enter into the city, merely approaching the gate and viewing around the twelve gates (if it were allowed or possible) will mean a world of pleasures and having a feeling of the immaculate best of the precious pearls with which the gates are made. All the riches in the world cannot afford a piece of them. Maybe the song that might spontaneously come out of the mouth of such a privileged fellow will be Psalm 100:4 (KJV), "Enter into his gates with thanksgiving, and into his courts with praise: be thankful unto him, and bless his name." Such a fellow might say, like King David, "For a day in thy courts is better than a thousand. I had rather be a doorkeeper in the house of my God, than to dwell in the tents of wickedness" (Psalm 84:10).

Staying around and admiring the beauty of the gates alone for years would have been more than enough satisfaction than living a thousand years on Earth with all the benefits that money, fame, popularity, and privilege could afford.

But certainly as the gates open unto the one who is most privileged to enter into the city, lo and behold, it is a shock to find out that the gates and all the pearls were child's play compared to the streets. "And the street of the city was pure gold, as it were transparent glass." (Revelation 21:21b).Not just ordinary gold, not imported gold from the best place in the universe, but brought into being in the purest form from the pure God for an everlasting abode of God, the angels, and the saints. If this fellow was an evangelist before he left the world, I bet he might be cut between two opinions. He may ask to plead to go back to the world in order to preach day and night all over the world, with all available resources as long as God will allow him, so that those who are yet to be qualified might by every means find grace and help to qualify to come to heaven. Or this evangelist might never want to look back, having had the opportunity of a lifetime to enter in once and for all eternity.

But perhaps he might choose the latter for fear of missing this once-in-a-lifetime opportunity. Everywhere he turns in the city is super golden, billions of times brighter than the Earth. In comparison to his former abode, it's like the whole Earth was full of darkness, where billions stumbled at the noonday sun. But here, nothing is hidden, "all things are bright and beautiful," and surely the Lord God made them all. God did not assign any angel to put them in place. Little wonder that this privileged fellow steps forward to see more of this place of unimaginable delight and utmost satisfaction.

The announcement to all would be possessors of the golden city is, "And there shall be no night there; and they need no candle, neither light of the sun; for the Lord God giveth them light: and they shall reign for ever and ever."(Revelation 22:5)

Imagine a place without any night, and everything therein is full of glamour, beauty, and pleasures all the way. Only the immortal God, the almighty Creator, can design such a place. This surely is the apex of desires. It's amazing that everything in heaven will be, in our common language, automatic because all the resources in heaven perpetually proceed from a God, who has no beginning or ending. He is never deficient of power or resources. He is all in all, and He has created all things, and for His pleasures they are and were created. "Moreover he doeth according to his will in the army of heaven, and among the inhabitants of the earth: and none can stay his hand, or say unto him, what doest thou?" (Daniel 4:6).

And now to the residential buildings, where the most privileged peoples from planet Earth will live forever. It's good news of great joy to hear about this from the King of the kingdom Himself, Jesus Christ, in John 14:1–3(KJV).

Let not your heart be troubled: ye believe in God, believe also in me. In my Father's house are many mansions: if it were not so, I would have told you. I go to prepare a place for you. And if I go and prepare a place for you, I will come again, and receive you unto myself; that where I am, there ye may be also.

Jesus did not make a promise of just buildings or houses but mansions! Glory to God. Even if Jesus had promised something like an apartment in heaven, it would still be amazingly more beautiful than any mansion on Earth. But more than that, He promises a mansion for every individual who will get to heaven.

Talk of the best of mansions built by the best architects and with the best materials. Talk of palaces with all that money can afford. Talk of estates with the latest technology. They cannot be compared to a doorknob of the mansions in heaven. Those mansions are beyond description within and without. It's hard to tell the shape, the width, the length, and the breadth of each of them. Their architectural designs are superbly matchless because they are built by the almighty God. It's no point trying to guess about all the beautiful things that will make up the building. But if Jesus says they are mansions, you can bet that the best ones on Earth will look like a filthy toilet in heaven.

THE TASTES OF THE
UTMOST PLEASURES

The Taste of the Utmost Pleasure of Freedom

The taste of the fullness of all pleasures starts with the transformation of the weak body, either at the Rapture of the saints or at the resurrection of the dead saints of God.

> So also is the resurrection of the dead. It is sown in corruption; it is raised in incorruption: It is sown in dishonor; it is raised in glory: it is sown in weakness; it is raised in power: It is sown a natural body; it is raised a spiritual body. There is a natural body, and there is a spiritual body.(1 Corinthians 15:42-44)

> And as we have borne the image of the earthy, we shall also bear the image of the heavenly (1Corinthians 15:49)

> For this corruptible must put on incorruption, and this mortal must put on immortality. In a moment, in the twinkling of an eye, at the last trump: for the trumpet shall sound, and the dead shall be raised incorruptible, and we shall be changed.

> So when this corruptible shall have put on incorruption,
> and this mortal shall have put on immortality, then shall
> be brought to pass the saying that is written, Death is
> swallowed up in victory. (1 Corinthians 15:53-54 KJV)

From that point, the body that was vulnerable to decay, weakness, corruption, temptation, pain, fear, limitation, and all sort of vices is put off forever. Now the believers will have bodies like angels and possess even the very image of Christ, as John the beloved revealed in 1 John 3:2 (KJV), "Beloved, now are we the sons of God, and it doth not yet appear what we shall be: but we know that, when he shall appear, we shall be like him; for we shall see him as he is."

What a bliss, what a freedom! It will then be free at last, and that for all eternity. So was God's desire, so was creation designed, even for pleasures of freedom, the true image of the Maker. It will be nothing short of eternal freedom.

What sort of freedom?

> There shall be freedom from the devil forever.
> There shall be freedom from all the
> works of the devil forever.
> There shall be freedom from sin,
> sicknesses, and self forever
> There shall be freedom from
> temptations and trials forever.
> There shall be freedom from any lack forever.
> There shall be freedom from fears
> of any nature forever.
> There shall be freedom from any
> form of failures forever.
> There shall be freedom from hell forever.
> There shall be freedom from death forever.
> There shall be freedom from any
> form of attacks forever.
> There shall be freedom from losses forever.

There shall be freedom sorrows,
sadness or loneliness forever.
There shall be freedom from any other desires forever.
There shall be freedom from any form of
oppression, injustice, or inequality forever.
There shall be freedom from the
wrath of God forever.
There shall be freedom from any
form of curse forever.
There shall be freedom from labors forever.
There shall be freedom from trials forever.
There shall be freedom from hatred forever.
There shall be freedom from limitations forever.
There shall be freedom from uncertainties forever.
There shall be full-fledged freedom for all eternity.

The Taste of the Utmost Pleasure of Rest

What a glorious rest it shall be in heaven. All who make it there shall have perpetual rest without measure. "There the wicked cease from troubling; and there the weary be at rest. There the prisoners rest together; they hear not the voice of the oppressor. The small and great are there; and the servant is free from his master" (Job 3:17–19).

Imagine having rest from any form of trouble whatsoever in a perpetual manner, whether from the devil, demons, principalities and powers, wicked men, or visible or invisible enemies.

Rest from natural disasters or otherwise.
Rest from woes, hues and cries.
Rest from disappointments and misunderstandings.
Rest from persecutions of any sort.
Rest from fear of tomorrow.
Rest from all forms of injustice.
Rest from failures or any form of reproaches.
Rest from labors and uncertainties.
Rest from searching for answers.

Rest from striving to make ends meet.

Rest from distresses and disasters.

Hebrews 4:9–10 (KJV) states, "There remaineth therefore a rest to the people of God. For he that is entered into his rest, he also hath ceased from his own works, as God did from his."

The Taste of the Utmost Pleasure of Peace

Making it to heaven after all the trials and temptations of life is an overwhelming pleasure of peace! Why? Even the best of saints still depend on the special grace and mercies of God to make it to heaven. Apostle Paul, in spite of all the exploits in the vineyard, with all the love exhibited, with all the humility displayed, with all the persecutions and trials endured, and with all the matchless labor in preaching, teaching, praying, fasting, admonishing, counseling, training, writing, and traveling here and there, says in 1 Corinthians 9:27 (KJV), "But I keep under my body, and bring it into subjection: lest that by any means, when I have preached to others, I myself should be a castaway."

He also warned those who are overconfident of making it in 1 Corinthians 10:12 (KJV), "Wherefore let him that thinketh he standeth take heed lest he fall."

He concluded in his letter to Jude and by extension to all believers, "Keep yourselves in the love of God, looking for the mercy of our Lord Jesus Christ unto eternal life" (Jude 1:21).

It is therefore not an understatement that invariably, it will take the mercies of God to make it to heaven. Christ said in *Matthew 7:13–14* (KJV),

Enter ye in at the strait gate: for wide is the gate, and broad is the way, that leadeth to destruction, and many there be which go in thereat: Because strait is the gate, and narrow is the way, which leadeth unto life, and few there be that find it."

Proverbs 21:31 (KJV) says, "The horse is prepared against the day of battle: but safety is of the LORD." And Romans 9:16 states, "So then it is not of him that willeth, nor of him that runneth, but of God that sheweth mercy."

Therefore stepping into the streets of gold will bring a sigh of great relief at last. There is peace of mind that through it all, there is now perpetual peace with God. Only here will be the true peace of God that passes all understanding. Nothing is ever stable on Earth: emotions change, desires change, environments change, people change, situations change, and somehow they affect the peace of even the best of believers. But upon stepping into heaven, where everything is in union with the Prince of Peace, all things are calm and perfectly controlled with undisturbed peace.

Three other scriptures that will make a believer who eventually makes it to heaven feel uncommon peace are also from Jesus. One is the story of the ten virgins, five being wise but five being foolish. Though virgins almost made it, some missed it by what could be said to be 1 percent. Nothing could be more painful and regrettable. Despite all the assurance and dedication as well as devotion, they were utterly disappointed. It all amounted to labor lost (Matthew 25).

The second is in Matthew 19:30, "But many that are first shall be last; and the last shall be first." The third is Matthew 7:21–23, "Not everyone that saith unto me, Lord, Lord, shall enter into the kingdom of heaven; but he that doeth the will of my Father which is in heaven. Many will say to me in that day, Lord, Lord, have we not prophesied in thy name? and in thy name have cast out devils? and in thy name done many wonderful works? And then will I profess unto them, I never knew you: depart from me, ye that work iniquity."

The first seconds of entering into heaven will mean peace, with uncountable beings residing there with one heart, one mind, one God, one Spirit, and perpetual oneness in everything and for all eternity.

What a heaven for the sheer pleasures of no fears of any kind. What a glorious peace that is.

No fear of trials, for there will be none.
No fear of death, for there will be none.
No fear of dangers, for there will be none.
No fear of sicknesses or afflictions,
for there will be none.
No fear of wicked peoples, for there will be none.

No fear of darkness, disappointments, enemies,
or failures, for there will be none.
No fear of anything by day, for there will be none.
No fear of lack, for there will be none.
No fear of temptations, for there
will be no devil to tempt.
No fear of losses, for there will be none.
No fear of disasters of any kind,
for there will be none.
No fear of hell, for there will be none.
No fear of ridicules, shame, or
oppressions, for there will be none.
No fear of judgments, for there will be none.
No fear of racism or prejudice, for there will be none.
No fear of death, for there will be none.

The Taste of the Utmost Pleasure of a Perfect State

> And God shall wipe away all tears from their eyes;
> and there shall be no more death, neither sorrow, nor
> crying, neither shall there be any more pain: for the
> former things are passed away. He that overcometh shall
> inherit all things; and I will be his God, and he shall be
> my son. (Revelation 21:6–7 KJV)

What else could these promises be called but the very perfect state
of God's pleasures? A state of life where you will never have any
reason to shed tears, whether you are young or old, for all eternity
is unimaginable. What a life! There will be no single reason to cry,
not even for a nanosecond, for all eternity! In heaven, the assurance
of no single moment of any situation or condition for shedding tears
is guaranteed. The inhabitants of heaven will definitely be like God,
and they will never experience aging talk less of dying due to old
age or diseases or attacks. The emotions in heaven are stable: joy is
stable, happiness is stable, and fellowship is stable. There shall never be
anything that brings sorrow of heart. No sorrowful events will ever

take place, but as it is written in Isaiah 51:11 (KJV), "Therefore the redeemed of the Lord shall return, and come with singing unto Zion; and everlasting joy shall be upon their head: they shall obtain gladness and joy; and sorrow and mourning shall flee away."

There shall never be a day of mourning.
There shall never be a day of pains.
There shall never be a day of anguish.
There shall never be a day of sadness.
There shall never be a day of disappointment.
There shall never be a day of weeping.
There shall be no accidents.
There shall be no injuries.
There shall be thefts.
There shall be no losses.
There shall be no emergencies.
There shall never be any ugly situation whatsoever.
There shall never be a day of any sickness.

Imagine how many sicknesses and diseases are in this world today: cancer, diabetes, heart disease, fever, cold, malaria, Alzheimer's and dementia, headaches. Not a single one is in heaven.

This is nothing short of pleasures par excellence.

As if that was not enough, God adds an incredible promise that in heaven, all things will be the portion of all believers who make it there. They shall inherit all things. How in the world does one explain having to inherit all things?

All things beautiful beyond expression.
All things wonderful beyond description.
All things pleasurable beyond ecstasy.
All things lovely.
All things pure.
All things perfect.
All things priceless.
All things peculiar.

All things joyful.
All things precious.
All things palatial.
All things praiseworthy.
All things enduring.
All things amazing.
All things glorious.
All things godly.
All things incomparable.
All things gracious.
All things peaceful
All things healthy.
All things adorable.
All things awesome.
All things charming.
All things dazzling.
All things excellent.
All things free.
All things fresh.
All things befitting.
All things honorable.
All things instantaneous.
All things impressive.
All things remarkable.
All things terrific.
All things thrilling.
All things valuable.
All things in abundance.
All things unedifying.
All things unfailing.
All things virtuous.

In fact, 1 Corinthians 2:9 (KJV) states, "But as it is written, Eye hath not seen, nor ear heard, neither have entered into the heart of man, the things which God hath prepared for them that love him."

The Taste of the Utmost Pleasure of New Things

> And he that sat upon the throne said, Behold, I make
> all things new. And he said unto me, Write: for these
> words are true and faithful. (Revelation 21:5)

All things being made new is another dimension to the pleasures of
God in heaven. The things God made at the beginning of creation had
the signature of the perfection of God's artistic ingenuity, and hence
He Himself said they were very good. But now He Himself promises
that He'll make all things new. If the first was very good and perfectly
designed, this new ones will be beyond expression in every dimension.
When God promises a new thing, the newness will be shocking in the
real sense of the word. It's like saying,

> For thus saith the Lord of hosts; yet once, it is a little
> while, and I will shake the heavens, and the earth, and
> the sea, and the dry land; And I will shake all nations,
> and the desire of all nations shall come: and I will fill
> this house with glory, saith the Lord of hosts. The silver
> is mine, and the gold is mine, saith the Lord of hosts.
> The glory of this latter house shall be greater than of the
> former, saith the Lord of hosts: and in this place will I
> give peace, saith the Lord of hosts. (Haggai 2:6-9)

Things will be so new that there will be nothing to compare
with everything that God will lavish on those in heaven. There will
no comparison in any form of experience before the inception a new
heaven and a new earth. There will be no comparison in the realm of
peace.

> There will be no comparison in the realm of joy.
> There will be no comparison in the realm of gladness.
> There will be no comparison in the realm of peace.
> There will be no comparison in the realm of love.
> There will be no comparison in the realm of unity.
> There will be no comparison in the realm of pleasures.

There will be no comparison in the realm of purity.
There will be no comparison in the realm of wealth.
There will be no comparison in the realm of status.
There will be no comparison in the realm of position.
There will be no comparison in the realm of longevity.
There will be no comparison in the realm of fullness.
There will be no comparison in the realm of satisfaction.

The Taste of the Utmost Pleasure of Seeing God

The manifestations of the works of God are awesome, but seeing God Himself is no doubt unspeakable joy and pleasure full of the highest glory. Seeing fathers Abraham, Isaac, and Jacob is more than a spectacle on its own! Walking side by side with Elijah, Elisha, David, Isaiah, Jeremiah, Ezekiel, and all the minor prophets will be nothing short of a great delight. Having wonderful fellowship with the apostles and all the other New Testament generals and saints is an abundance of indescribable joy. Coming face-to-face with the innumerable angels of God will be beyond ecstatic. But think about seeing the almighty God, the maker of heaven and the Earth; the omnipotent, omniscient, and omnipresent; the I Am that I Am; the Alpha and Omega; the very King of glory who was, who is, will forever be like billions of pleasures raised to unlimited power throughout eternity.

Here is the sure promise in Revelation 21:3–5.

> And there shall be no more curse: but the throne of God and of the Lamb shall be in it; and his servants shall serve him: And they shall see his face; and his name shall be in their foreheads. And there shall be no night there; and they need no candle, neither light of the sun; for the Lord God giveth them light: and they shall reign for ever and ever.

Songwriters Carolyn Cross and Phil Cro wrote,

> One day will overflow
> I'm gonna let the glory roll when the
> Roll is called in Glory
> I'll gonna get beside myself when I get
> Beside the King that day
> I'm gonna have the time of my life
> When the time of my life is over
> I'm gonna get carried away when I get
> Carried away

The group Mercy Me penned,

> I can only imagine what it will be like
> When I walk, by your side
> I can only imagine what my eyes will see
> When your face is before me
> …
> Surrounded by Your glory
> What will my heart feel
> …
> I can only imagine when all I would do is forever
> Forever worship You

Generations have read, heard, thought, and philosophized about this God. Wars have been fought about Him, and many had been oppressed, guillotined, sawn asunder, stoned, imprisoned, set on fire alive, thrown into the mouths of lions, hacked, beheaded, poisoned, drowned, betrayed, tormented and tortured, and hung on trees for the name of God. Countless books, literary works, tracts, sermons, teachings, conferences, seminars, trainings, prayers, fastings, self-denials, reproaches, and the like have been done in the name of God. How about prophecies, visions, and dreams from generation to generation? How many songs had been composed? How many wars and rumors of wars? How many countless arguments? Debates and productive and counterproductive events? Misgivings and misunderstandings? Manipulations and malpractices? Truths and lies? Doctrines and dogmas? True prophets and fake prophets? All of these in the name of this God.

It's been said He never exists, and there are numerous concepts and religions professing the knowledge of God.

> **Bahá'í:** Followers of the Bahá'í faith believe in one God, who is omnipotent, perfect, has complete knowledge of life and that the universe and all creations belong to Him/Her.

> **Buddhism:** Buddhists do not believe in a God or gods.

> **Jainism:** The Jain religion does not have any gods or spiritual beings.

> **Islam:** Muslims believe that there is only one God, and that is Allah.

> **Mormonism:** Believe that God is a perfect, exalted man with a physical body.

> **Judaism:** Believed to be the original of the three Abrahamic faiths, which also include Christianity and Islam, and the followers of this religion are known as Jews. They believe that there is only one God who can't be subdivided into different persons, unlike in Christianity.

> **Christianity:** Christians believe in one God. According to Christianity, Jesus Christ is the Son of God.

> **Hinduism:** Known to be "a family of religions" because it has no single founder or scripture and no commonly agreed set of teachings.

Rastafarianism or Rastafari: A religion that believes in one God named Jah. They believe that Haile Selassie I, the king of Ethiopia who was crowned in 1930, was the physical manifestation of God on Earth.

Confucianism: Propagated by the Chinese philosopher Kung Fu Tzu, better known as Confucius. The religion does not have a God and is focused on bringing harmony to individuals and to society.

Shinto: A Japanese religion that has no God and no founder. However, it lays a lot of emphasis on rituals and devotion to kami, which are invisible spiritual beings and powers connected to humans.

Sikhism: Founded by Guru Nanak and based on his teachings. They believe that there is only one God and that it is without form or gender. Everyone has direct access to this God.

Taoism: Rooted in Chinese customs, Taoism is about the Tao, which is a concept that defines the ultimate creative principle of the universe, not God. Followers worship several deities in Taoist temples.

Zoroastrianism: Founded by the Prophet Zoroaster (or Zarathustra). They believe that there is only one God, called Ahura Mazda (meaning Wise Lord), who has no form, and humans cannot comprehend Him.

Agnosticism: Belief that God, if it exists, is by nature unknowable and will always be unknowable.

Animism: The belief that all objects contain spirits.

Atheism: Active and extrinsic disbelief that God exists.

Mysticism: Belief that God is unknowable but accessible.

Eckankar: Belief a person's soul can escape the physical body and travel freely within other planes of reality. They take God as divine Spirit.

Satanism: An atheist religion that uses dark and evil symbology.

Scientology: Belief in reincarnation.

When all is said and done, with all proofs and disproofs, at the end of the day, the only true God will be visible to all who make it to heaven. Seeing God and being with Him for eternity is the climax of all pleasures. Psalm 16:11 (KJV) says, "Thou wilt shew me the path of life: in thy presence is fullness of joy; at thy right hand there are pleasures for evermore."

Being a God of pleasures Himself, there cannot be anything less for all who make it to His presence.

Seeing God is the pleasure of pleasures.
Seeing God is the apex of all the
other goodies in heaven.
Seeing God is the highest attainment
of any created being.
Seeing God is the highest preoccupation
for any created being.
Seeing God is the highest honor for all eternity.
Seeing God is the highest of all
glories eyes can behold.
Seeing God is wishing for nothing
else to see for all eternity.
Seeing God makes other things in heaven less
valuable, even though they are still highly precious.
Seeing God makes all other beings anywhere
and everywhere stand still in awe.

Seeing God becomes the highest preoccupation
of unending adoration and worship.
Seeing God provokes continuous highest praises and
thanksgiving.

After this I looked, and, behold, a door was opened
in heaven: and the first voice which I heard was as it
were of a trumpet talking with me; which said, Come
up hither, and I will shew thee things which must be
hereafter.[2] And immediately I was in the spirit: and,
behold, a throne was set in heaven, and one sat on the
throne. And he that sat was to look upon like a jasper
and a sardine stone: and there was a rainbow round
about the throne, in sight like unto an emerald.

And round about the throne were four and twenty
seats: and upon the seats I saw four and twenty elders
sitting, clothed in white raiment; and they had on their
heads crowns of gold. And out of the throne proceeded
lightnings and thunderings and voices: and there were
seven lamps of fire burning before the throne, which
are the seven Spirits of God.

And before the throne there was a sea of glass like
unto crystal: and in the midst of the throne, and round
about the throne, were four beasts full of eyes before
and behind.

And the first beast was like a lion, and the second beast
like a calf, and the third beast had a face as a man, and
the fourth beast was like a flying eagle.

And the four beasts had each of them six wings about
him; and they were full of eyes within: and they rest
not day and night, saying, Holy, holy, holy, Lord God
Almighty, which was, and is, and is to come.[9] And when

those beasts give glory and honour and thanks to him
that sat on the throne, who liveth for ever and ever,

The four and twenty elders fall down before him that sat
on the throne, and worship him that liveth for ever and
ever, and cast their crowns before the throne, saying,

Thou art worthy, O Lord, to receive glory and honour
and power: for thou hast created all things, and for thy
pleasure they are and were created. (Revelation 4:1–11)

The Taste of the Utmost Pleasure of Music

The role of music from age to age has been amazing. Music is magically
enchanting, uplifting, enjoyable, cheerful, soothing, pleasant, satisfying,
and pleasurable. All kinds of instruments accompany various music
genres. The rhythms they produce superbly delight listeners and
captivate their entire being. Well, that's the music on Earth, which is
by no means perfectly rendered. Even the award-winning ones on Earth
cannot be compared to that of heaven, where everything is flawless.
When angels, which are perfect beings, take up perfect instruments in
heaven to lead songs of worship and adoration, how will one describe
that in human language?

And when he had taken the book, the four beasts and
four and twenty elders fell down before the Lamb,
having every one of them harps, and golden vials full
of odours, which are the prayers of saints.

And they sung a new song, saying, Thou art worthy
to take the book, and to open the seals thereof: for
thou wast slain, and hast redeemed us to God by thy
blood out of every kindred, and tongue, and people,
and nation;

And hast made us unto our God kings and priests: and we shall reign on the earth.

And I beheld, and I heard the voice of many angels round about the throne and the beasts and the elders: and the number of them was ten thousand times ten thousand, and thousands of thousands;

Saying with a loud voice, worthy is the Lamb that was slain to receive power, and riches, and wisdom, and strength, and honour, and glory, and blessing. (Revelation 5:8-12)

It's beyond imaginations when millions sing harmoniously together to worship the almighty God in the beauty of holiness.

Another reference is also made to picture how glorious music will be in heaven

And I heard a voice from heaven, as the voice of many waters, and as the voice of a great thunder: and I heard the voice of harpers harping with their harps: And they sung as it were a new song before the throne, and before the four beasts, and the elders: and no man could learn that song but the hundred and forty and four thousand, which were redeemed from the earth. (Revelation 14:2-3)

New songs will be rendered continuously in heaven. Everyone will be fully satisfied with the perfect melodies billions of times better than the best songs or melodies ever rendered since the beginning of the world by all the best artists put together.

And I saw as it were a sea of glass mingled with fire: and them that had gotten the victory over the beast, and over his image, and over his mark, and over the number of his name, stand on the sea of glass, having the harps of God.

And they sing the song of Moses the servant of God, and the song of the Lamb, saying, great and marvelous are thy works, Lord God Almighty; just and true are thy ways, thou King of saints.

Who shall not fear thee, O Lord, and glorify thy name? For thou only art holy: for all nations shall come and worship before thee; for thy judgments are made manifest. (Revelation 15:2–4)

The Taste of the Utmost Pleasure of Fellowship

The Bible says in *Psalm 133:1–3 (KJV)*,

Behold, how good and how pleasant it is for brethren to dwell together in unity!

It is like the precious ointment upon the head that ran down upon the beard even Aaron's beard: that went down to the skirts of his garments;

As the dew of Hermon, and as the dew that descended upon the mountains of Zion: for there the Lord commanded the blessing, even life for evermore.

This was the expectation among imperfect believers on Earth. While on Earth, though redeemed, there are manifestations of individual emotions, individual ways of thinking and acting, individual desires, and individual weaknesses that may not be sinful but may not allow for a perfect unity. But in heaven, there shall be perfect unison of all things with God, the maker of all things. What a glorious fellowship in heaven with God the Father, God the Son, God the Holy Ghost, all myriads of angels, and innumerable saints.

In this world, there are many great men and women, especially children of God, whom we would love to see face-to-face, dine with, and fellowship with, but they came in different dispensations, and we only read or heard about them. Some are in the same generation, but it was not possible to see them or meet with them, much less have fellowship with them. But in heaven, there will be full view of all saints from the Old Testament to the New Testament. Saints of God in every generation since the world began till the end of age shall be in everlasting fellowship in the same vicinity.

> After this I beheld, and, lo, a great multitude, which no man could number, of all nations, and kindreds, and people, and tongues, stood before the throne, and before the Lamb, clothed with white robes, and palms in their hands. (Revelation 7:9)

What a delight and pure pleasure to fellowship with fathers Abraham, Isaac, and Jacob. There on the other side is Joseph and all his brothers, with no remembrance of old Egypt (all things have become new). Oh! Here comes Prophet Moses, the man of God, perhaps sharing with Aaron, Miriam, Caleb, and Joshua, recounting the experiences of the past while on their way to the Promised Land. Perhaps Moses will be full of gratitude to God that in spite of not stepping into the earthly Canaan, there is now no regret because the heavenly one is by no means comparable to the earthly one. Joshua might also narrate that he thought the greatest achievement of his life was getting to the earthly Promised Land, but now he realizes that getting to heaven is a billion times more of an achievement than any earthly achievements and endeavors.

If by chance Joseph hears that Moses and Caleb are looking back to all the exploits and achievements on earth, he might also chip in some words, saying that he thought the best favor from God was the greatness and the pleasures of being a ruler of the entire land of Egypt, but now the reality is that he would rather lie on the streets in a corner in heaven than have all the privileges he enjoyed on Earth. How about sighting Prophet Samuel rejoicing with other prophets like Isaiah, Jeremiah, Ezekiel, and more, both inside and outside the Bible? Prophet Jonah might echo the New Testament declaration in Titus 2:11–3:8 (KJV), particularly "for the grace of God that bringeth salvation hath appeared to all men," as he recognizes some saints from Nineveh among the multitudes from all over the nations of the world rejoicing in heaven.

It's an amazing privilege throughout eternity to company with great prophets like Elijah and Elisha. If there could be any room to poke a little fun with Prophet Elisha, how dare he run from a woman after destroying four hundred priests of Baal? Or how come he ate the food from the angels when he asked for death? How was the taste of the meal brought by a raven? One might ask about the paradox of Elijah's bone raising a dead man while he himself died of sickness! Of course, joy will overshadow all the events of old. Now all things are new, all things are understood, and all things are positive.

It will be a beautiful fellowship to have the array of some kings who eventually make it to heaven too. Standing out among them will be King David recalling, "For a day in thy courts is better than a thousand. I had rather be a doorkeeper in the house of my God, than to dwell in the tents of wickedness" (Psalm 84:10–12 KJV). But this time around, he might want to say not only "to dwell in the tents of wickedness" but "than to be in the best palaces in the entire world."

What a sweet fellowship with the likes of Mary, the mother of the Lord and Savior, Jesus Christ! The glory of Christ now, the majesty of Christ now, and the adoration of Christ now, in contradistinction to how, He being God, conditioned Himself and subjected Himself into the womb of a mortal woman on Earth and tasted of human frailty so He could be the savior of all humankind, now makes sense. What an amazing array of women like Ruth, Deborah, Elizabeth, Esther, and Dorcas. And lest we forget the lovely maid in Namaan, the leper's house, and many other servants with no names on Earth. But now they share the glory in heaven with kings and queens to show that "Of a truth I perceive that God is no respecter of persons: But in every nation he that feareth him, and worketh righteousness, is accepted with him" (Acts10:35).

Here comes jubilant Paul, perhaps hand in hand with Peter, the Rock, and Barnabas and other apostles, narrating that it was worth it all to have suffered and be given the privilege to spread the light of the gospel and suffer for Christ. Maybe Paul might be allowed to say it loud and clear again,

> But what things were gain to me, those I counted loss for Christ. Yea doubtless, and I count all things but loss for the excellency of the knowledge of Christ Jesus my Lord: for whom I have suffered the loss of all things, and do count them but dung, that I may win Christ,
>
> And be found in him, not having mine own righteousness, which is of the law, but that which is through the faith of Christ, the righteousness which is of God by faith:
>
> That I may know him, and the power of his resurrection, and the fellowship of his sufferings, being made conformable unto his death;
>
> If by any means I might attain unto the resurrection of the dead. (Philippians 3:7–11)

But now rephrasing the last sentence, "now we have obtained the resurrection of the dead," the theology is a reality.

What a sweet and wonderful fellowship, what a joy divine, seeing all saints from all the continents.

All are fashioned alike as one heavenly nation, united together forever in mind, and in outlook, in fellowship with angels and God Himself. In appreciation to the sacrifice of Jesus Christ, who made it possible for everyone to partake in this glorious and everlasting fellowship, the hymn of gratitude might be sung with the backing of the trumpets of angels.

> In tenderness He sought me,
> Weary and sick with sin,
> And on His shoulders brought me
> Back to His fold again.

...

O the love that sought me!
O the blood that bought me!
O the grace that brought me to the fold,
Wondrous grace that brought me to the fold!

—W. Spencer Walton, 1894

This type of fellowship was the pleasure designed by God to bind us together in perpetual love. All things are harmoniously bound together. The original fellowship at the cool of the day, with God and Adam and Eve in the peaceful and flourishing Garden of Eden, was God's design. He never designed chaos, He never designed disruption, He never designed acrimony, and He never designed disunity. All He created and designed was originally very good and for the good of all creatures.

The Taste of the Utmost Pleasure of Orderliness

Let all things be done decently and in order. (1 Corinthians 14:40 KJV).

There is no doubting the fact that God is a God of order—hence being who He is, He desires that everything without any exception should be in order.

He created the heaven and earth in order.
He created the galaxies in order.
He placed the stars, the moon, and the sun in order.
He created the Garden of Eden in order.
He created the light and divided the
light from darkness in order.
He called the light day and the
darkness night all in order.
He brought in water and made them
come together in order.

He commanded up the dry land to
form the Earth in order.
He made the earth to bring forth grass,
herbs, and trees, yielding fruits in order.
He commanded the waters to bring
forth moving creatures in order.
He made the earth bring forth
living creatures in order.
He crowned the creation with man
to have dominion in order.
He made man fearfully and wonderfully
with all the intricacies in order.

The head with brain to think and the ears to ear. The nostrils to
smell, the eyes to see. The face, the eyebrows, and hairs for beauty.
The eyelashes to shield. The set of teeth to chew, bite, and crack (and
to laugh). The tongue to taste and coordinate speech. The arms to do
manifold things. The legs to walk, run, jump, and kick. The bones,
veins, marrow, and other internal organs in their layers to coordinate
the affairs of the massive body.

The God of order made water and blood to make the body function.
The center of it all is the heart, where resides the breath of life. He
made them all in order. "So God created man in his own image, in
the image of God created he him; male and female created he them"
(Genesis 1:27 KJV).

All the aforementioned and much more are proof that God is indeed
a God of orderliness. This was no doubt part of His pleasure. However,
things got out of order when Adam and Eve fell in the Garden of Eden.
Corruption and all other vices came in at the end of the day.

And God saw that the wickedness of man was great in
the earth, and that every imagination of the thoughts
of his heart was only evil continually.

And it repented the Lord that he had made man on the
earth, and it grieved him at his heart. And the Lord said,

> I will destroy man whom I have created from the face of
> the earth; both man, and beast, and the creeping thing,
> and the fowls of the air; for it repenteth me that I have
> made them. (Genesis 6:5–7)

Full and perpetual orderliness will never be regained until the new heaven and new Earth emerge. Hence the proclamation in Revelation 21:5, "And he that sat upon the throne said, Behold, I make all things new."

All who dwell in heaven will have the utmost pleasure of orderliness in all spheres of life for all eternity.

> The weather will be in order.
> The emotions of everyone will be in order.
> The will of everyone will be in order.
> The motion of all things will be in order.
> The language, relationships, and interactions will be
> in order.
> Mode of worship will be in order.
> Mode of fellowship will be in order.
> Mode of reasoning will be in order
> Mode of actions will be in order.
> Mode of responses will be in order.
> Mode of greetings will be in order.
> Mode of services will be in order.
> Mode of music will be in order.
> Mode of all conducts will be in order.
> Mode of movements will be in order.
> Mode of communication will be in order.
> Mode of operation of all things will be in order.
> Who does what, when, and how will be in order.
> Who gets what, when, and how will be in order.
> What comes, when, and how will be in order.
> What happens, when, and how will be in order.

In fact, the utmost pleasures of all things being done decently and in order will be the hallmark of all things in heaven for everyone to enjoy. It was said that when the queen of Sheba visited Solomon,

> And when the queen of Sheba had seen all Solomon's wisdom, and the house that he had built, And the meat of his table, and the sitting of his servants, and the attendance of his ministers, and their apparel, and his cupbearers, and his ascent by which he went up unto the house of the Lord; there was no more spirit in her. And she said to the king, It was a true report that I heard in mine own land of thy acts and of thy wisdom. Howbeit I believed not the words, until I came, and mine eyes had seen it: and, behold, the half was not told me: thy wisdom and prosperity exceedeth the fame which I heard. Happy are thy men, happy are these thy servants, which stand continually before thee, and that hear thy wisdom. Blessed be the Lord thy God, which delighted in thee, to set thee on the throne of Israel: because the Lord loved Israel forever, therefore made he thee king, to do judgment and justice. (1 Kings 10:5–9)

But Jesus Christ says, "A greater than Solomon is here" (Luke 11:31 KJV). If the Queen of Sheba could so glorify the earthly kingdom of Solomon with respect to the orderliness of all things, what greatness par excellence shall be the order of things in the kingdom of heaven, where everything is superbly incomparable in beauty, glamour, and orderliness?

The Taste of the Utmost Pleasure of Rewards

> And, behold, I come quickly; and my reward is with me, to give every man according as his work shall be. (Revelation 22:12)

> Therefore, my beloved brethren, be ye stedfast, unmoveable, always abounding in the work of the Lord,

forasmuch as ye know that your labour is not in vain in the Lord. (1 Corinthians 15:58)

It's the height of joy and glory on Earth to be a winner in major events, especially when there are other great competitors. Think about the glory of sportsmen and women who are champions in their own right, winning gold medals while being cheered to victories by millions of spectators. What a feeling of great joy for their accomplishments, for the honors, for the rewards in cash, trophies, medals, popularity, and other benefits. Their names become household names, and the media display them around the world. They also attract many followers to whom they become heroes or heroines. Their names are immortalized in halls of fame. Their nations, families, and friends are so proud of them, and they are almost revered. Great as these are on Earth, and as wonderful as all the accolades might look, the Bible says, "Know ye not that they which run in a race run all, but one receiveth the prize? So run, that ye may obtain. And every man that striveth for the mastery is temperate in all things. Now they do it to obtain a corruptible crown; but we an incorruptible" (1 Corinthians 9:24–25). In other words, whatever the glory, accomplishments, ovations, triumphs, or pleasure of victories in this world, it's just for a period of time, transient and corruptible, in comparison to the pleasures of the rewards in heaven that will be enjoyed for all eternity.

And I heard as it were the voice of a great multitude, and as the voice of many waters, and as the voice of mighty thunderings, saying, Alleluia: for the Lord God omnipotent reigneth. Let us be glad and rejoice, and give honour to him: for the marriage of the Lamb is come, and his wife hath made herself ready.

And to her was granted that she should be arrayed in fine linen, clean and white: for the fine linen is the righteousness of saints. And he saith unto me, Write, Blessed are they which are called unto the marriage

supper of the Lamb. And he saith unto me, these are the
true sayings of God. (Revelation 19:6–9)

There shall be numerous rewards in heaven for believers at the
Bema Seat: crowns, mansions, new names, white stones, and more—all
of these in the presence of multitude of saints and angels. That will be
wonder of wonders. Entering into heaven to live with God, all saints,
and the angels is more than a reward, but this is in addition to other
special rewards that are incomparable in nature and honor with that
of the world. It will be of tremendous pleasure to witness the awards
ceremony and also be a receiver. By this, the glory of God and His
worship will soar higher because this is how He designed all things to
be. What a pleasure that will be for all the residents in heaven to have
this memory kept forever.

The Taste of the Utmost Pleasure of New Food and Drink

But I say unto you, I will not drink henceforth of this
fruit of the vine, until that day when I drink it new with
you in my Father's kingdom. (Matthew 26:29)

For the Lamb which is in the midst of the throne shall
feed them, and shall lead them unto living fountains
of waters: and God shall wipe away all tears from their
eyes. (Revelation 7:17 KJV)

It will be an amazing pleasure to drink and eat in heaven. We know how
it feels to have a taste of the best drink or food with the right appetite
and good health, even here on earth. What satisfaction do we derive
from such? As if one should say, "Give us this bread evermore" (John
6:34), but after awhile, one is fed up with it. But in heaven, everything
is perfect. Perfect appetite, perfect taste, perfect mood, perfect company,
perfect drinks, and perfect variety of food.

How will they look? How will they taste like? Who will be the
cook? One thing is certain: because all things will be made totally new,

there will be none like the drinks and the food in heaven compared to those on earth. The food of kings and rulers of this world are always sumptuous. How much better will be the food of the King of kings and Lord of lords? Christ is the King of the kingdom of God, so He will be the one to serve the people of God and also dine with them with the host of angels. It can be concluded that the taste and the pleasures that will be derived from them shall be beyond human expression.

The Taste of the Utmost Pleasure of Spirituality

> Beloved, now are we the sons of God, and it doth not
> yet appear what we shall be: but we know that, when
> he shall appear, we shall be like him; for we shall see
> him as he is. (1 John 3:2–3 KJV)

Doubtless, all the saints of God will have glorified bodies, weather raptured or resurrected from the dead. It goes without saying that the nature of all saints in heaven will be a perfect state, like the nature of God. There shall be no single struggle with attainment to the highest state of spirituality. Once in heaven, there are no spiritual mountains to climb anymore. All that needs to be known is now a reality.

There shall be no falling and rising in all the components and characteristics of a spiritual being. Angels are spiritual beings, God is also a spiritual being (John 4:24–26).

> There shall be no more Bible studies.
> There shall be no more prayer meetings.
> There shall be no more seminars or seminaries.
> There shall be no more pastors,
> teachers, evangelists, or prophets.
> There shall be no more fasting.
> There shall be no more tongues or
> interpretation of tongues.
> There shall be no more manifestations
> of the gifts of the Spirit.

"God is a Spirit: and they that worship him must worship him in spirit and in truth (John 4:24 KJV). All the fruit of the Spirit will be in full manifestation in all the inhabitants of heaven. "But the fruit of the Spirit is love, joy, peace, longsuffering, gentleness, goodness, faith, Meekness, temperance: against such there is no law" (Galatians 5:22–23).

All creatures will be fully clothed with the glory of God. They will be full of holiness and righteousness forever. They will be eternally secured with power and authority. This is also a reminder of the state of man when he was originally created. Genesis 1:27 (KJV) states, "So God created man in his own image, in the image of God created he him; male and female created he them." Ephesians 4:24 (KJV) explains this further: "And that ye put on the new man, which after God is created in righteousness and true holiness."

In heaven, the echo of the original design rings, but something greater and higher is manifested. The fact remains that the very desire of God to fulfill the purpose "all things were created for His pleasure and they are" becomes a full reality that all things were ultimately designed for pleasures.

The Taste of Utmost Perfection of the Senses

It is widely recognized that there are undeniable various senses through which pleasures or displeasures are pronounced:

> The sense of touch.
> The sense of sight.
> The sense of hearing.
> The sense of smell.
> The sense of taste.

In the biblical arena, faith is said to be the higher expression of all the senses. All the five aforementioned senses may not be involved, yet faith is active and required in a believer on Earth. However, this will terminate upon getting to heaven because all that's hoped for will become perfect reality. Hebrews 11:1 (KJV) states, "Now faith is the substance of things hoped for, the evidence of things not seen."

What you touch affects you. What you see affects you. What you hear definitely affects you. What you smell affects you, as well as what you taste. Of course there are other discovered senses, but we'll limit ourselves to these to buttress godly pleasures. This has little or nothing to do with the Epicurean principles (devotion to pleasure, comfort, and high living, with a certain nicety of style), which was based on human philosophy only and not on divine purpose of God. However, without all these senses being active, pleasures and displeasures are completely dead and of no effect, whether on Earth or in heaven. If there are no feelings, then there are no pains or pleasures. God put them in His creature for the purpose of expression of displeasures or pleasure. All that the Creator designed is meant for good pleasures in God's own environment, with divine principles that run through them.

The Ultimate Sense of Touch

How wonderful it feels to touch and be touched with loving hands. Think about loving hands holding cute babies, or of loving hands of spouses walking to the altar, together by the garden, together in the house, and together in privacy. How about loving hugs in fellowship or the bond of two becoming one (husband and wife) during intimacy? Or high-fives to show an expression of acknowledgment and affirmation of kudos? The shaking of other people's hands as a gesture of fellowship and love? The holy and romantic kisses as an expression of true and pure romantic love?

All these are great feelings here on Earth when rightly displayed. Even though they are short-lived, they are nonetheless powerful and wonderful experiences of joy and goodness.

These are nothing compared to the touch from saints in heaven, angels in heaven, the almighty God, the Father, the Son, and the Holy Ghost. The feelings of the touch of all these entities and many more that are yet unknown shall not only be amazing but also linger not only for few minutes or few years but for all eternity in heaven.

The Ultimate Sense of Smell

When the Lord promised to make all things new, he did not exclude the sense of smell. In fact, it will be in a perfect state. The freshness of the entire heaven will be amazing.

> Never any smell of pollution therein.
> Never any laundering therein.
> Never any dead or buried stuff therein.
> Never any pollution or pollutant therein.
> Never any human or animal waste therein.
> Never any dust therein.
> Never any bad breath therein.
> Never any decay therein.
> Never any Dead Sea or lakes therein.
> Never any rotten elements therein.
> Never any garbage therein.

Everything in heaven is alive and fresh, and it will remain so forever.

> The flowers are alive and perfect.
> The beings are alive and perfect.
> The trees are alive and perfect.
> The mansions will smell fresh forever.
> Rivers will smell fresh forever.
> The air will smell fresh forever.
> The flowers will smell fresh forever.

The times of refreshing that were promised will be in full manifestation.

> Freshness of the mind.
> Freshness of the spirit.
> Freshness of reunion.
> Freshness of fellowship.
> Freshness of worship.
> Freshness of days without a single night.
> Freshness of all the beauties in heaven.

Freshness of the presence of God.
Freshness of spiritual well-being.

It's the place of life in abundance and in its fullness, and hence the sense of smell will experience enjoyable perfect freshness of everything for all eternity. What a great sense of pleasure that will be.

The Ultimate Sense of Taste

Let's rest on the validity of the scriptures:

> But I say unto you, I will not drink henceforth of this fruit of the vine, until that day when I drink it new with you in my Father's kingdom. (Matthew 26:29)

> They shall hunger no more, neither thirst anymore; neither shall the sun light on them, nor any heat. For the Lamb which is in the midst of the throne shall feed them, and shall lead them unto living fountains of waters: and God shall wipe away all tears from their eyes. (Revelation 7:16–17)

It is certain there will be continuous sense of taste. Nothing else can be compared with the perfect sense of taste, perfect health, perfect heart, perfect environment, and personification of perfection Himself, Jesus Christ, feeding the saints and drinking with us in heaven. How can a mortal man describe such?

The Ultimate Sense of Sight

Apostle Paul captured the attention of would-be inhabitants of heaven in a very graphic yet amazing way beyond human imagination with respect to what the ultimate sense of sight will look like in 1 Corinthians 2:9 (KJV), "But as it is written, Eye hath not seen, nor ear heard, neither have entered into the heart of man, the things which God hath prepared for them that love him."

In other words, what we shall see in heaven is beyond the realm of the entire universe in beauty, in scope, in majesty, in splendor, in richness, in glory, in brightness, in design, in colors, in radiance, in attraction, in aesthetics, in multifacetedness, in awesomeness. The more you see, the more the glory!

> Perfect sight of God and His majestic glory.
> Perfect sight of the throne of God.
> Perfect sight of the streets of gold.
> Perfect sight of gorgeous mansions.
> Perfect sight of all saints and angels in beautiful garments
> and glorified bodies.
> Perfect sight of nature at the best.
> Perfect sight of the glory of the entire environment.

Then shall the hymn "How Beautiful Heaven Must Be" by George Joes become a reality.

> We read of a place that's called heaven,
> It's made for the pure and the free;
> These truths in God's word He has given,
> How beautiful heaven must be.
>
> How beautiful heaven must be
> Sweet home of the happy and free;
> Fair haven of rest for the weary,
> How beautiful heaven must be.

The Ultimate Sense of Hearing

Let's talk about a place where there will be no noise at all, but every sound and voice heard in heaven will be sweet to all hearers. Think about the sound of music, of trumpets, of whatever other instruments might be used. How about the voices of multitudes, all in perfect harmony? Every move and every sound will be perfectly interpreted and perfectly decoded. There shall be no single thing defective there, and neither shall there be any form of misunderstanding.

To crown it all, hearing the voice of God, the voice of angels, and the voices of the saints will be altogether awesome. Every day for all eternity will be good news. No news of death, no news of pains, no news of sorrows, no news of accidents, no news of bad weather, no news of oppression, no news of tragedy, no news of accidents, no news of famine, no news of confusion, no news of change of government, no news of bad economy, no news of a better county. Then shall the scriptures be fulfilled: "Therefore the redeemed of the Lord shall return, and come with singing unto Zion; and everlasting joy shall be upon their head: they shall obtain gladness and joy; and sorrow and mourning shall flee away" (Isaiah 51:11 KJV). These certainly are the pleasures of the almighty God.

The Taste of Utmost Pleasure of Love

> Charity [LOVE] never faileth: but whether there be prophecies, they shall fail; whether there be tongues, they shall cease; whether there be knowledge, it shall vanish away. (1 Corinthians 13:8)

It's only in heaven that the utmost, purest, perfect, unstoppable love will be fully experienced. In the present circumstances in this world, sometimes our expression of love is not stable and not really full. Our love for one another even as brethren, our love for the our families, and our love for other peoples change from time to time due to human frailty, shortcomings, and misunderstandings. It is shocking but true that even our love for God sometimes is not on the same level. We somehow feel God is far from us.

> Behold, I go forward, but he is not there; and backward, but I cannot perceive him on the left hand, where he doth work, but I cannot behold him: he hideth himself on the right hand, that I cannot see him).

> Sometimes we only quote it by faith, but the substance seems elusive. (Job 23:8–9)

Sometimes there is doubt, and other times there is seemingly fullness of assurance.

> Why do we cry sometimes?
> Why do we lament sometimes?
> Why do we complain sometimes?
> Why do we pray in the real sense of the word?
> Why do we sometimes feel like giving up?
> Why do we need motivations, encouragement and exhortations?
> Why not on the same mountaintop of love all the time?

Well, the answer is, "For we know in part, and we prophesy in part. But when that which is perfect is come, then that which is in part shall be done away" (1 Corinthians 13:9–10).

The taste of the utmost pleasure of love will be experienced in heaven for all eternity.

> It will be love without measures.
> It will be love without conditions.
> It will be love without contradictions.
> It will be love without considerations.
> It will be love without misunderstanding.
> It will be love without boundaries.
> It will be love on the same level to all and from all.
> It will be love most perpetual.
> It will be love freely expressed.
> It will be love most heartfelt.
> It will be love on sight and out of sight.
> It will be love for everything and through everything.

It will be love beyond anything ever experienced by anyone until then. Here in this world, it is not possible to love everyone equally, or for everyone to love you even if you love them. But the fascinating thing about the love that will be expressed in heaven is that it will be possible for the millions of people in heaven to love you equally, and vice visa. Imagine receiving the same measure of love from millions of people at the same time—and you having the capacity to love them to the same degree. There shall be peoples from all nations of the world and from all generations in heaven. The most outstanding thing that will permeate the atmosphere of heaven for all eternity is the expression of love in the purest form.

The expression of God's love will be fully felt.

Everything in heaven will breathe in and breathe out love.

> The faces of all saints will show forth love.
> The faces of all angels will show forth love.
> The face of God the Father will show forth love.
> The face of God the Son will show forth love.
> The face of God the Holy Spirit will show forth love.

All who are in heaven are made of love because God is love. Hence the mansions are the expression of love.

> The gates are the expression of love.
> The flowers are the expression of love.
> The services are the expression of love.
> The rewards are the expression of love.
> The streets of gold are the expression of love.
> The trees are the expression of love.
> The throne of God is the expression of love.
> The music is the expression of love.
> The instruments are the expression of love.
> The fellowship will be an expression of love.
> Nothing in heaven will lack the expression of love.

It is needful to point out that there will be no romantic love in heaven, because there will be no marriage or giving in marriage. Matthew 22:30 (KJV) states, "For in the resurrection they neither marry, nor are given in marriage, but are as the angels of God in heaven." However, the highest form of love, which drowns every other form of expression of love, will be the pleasure of all inhabitants of heaven throughout eternity.

In short, everything and everyone in heaven will be overflowing with the expression of love in the magnitude never imagined. It will fully and for all eternity bring one to fulfillment.

> And now abideth faith, hope, charity,(love) these three; but the greatest of these is charity (love). (1 Corinthians 13: 13)

Nine

---∽---

PERVERSE PLEASURES

"But she that liveth in pleasure is dead while she liveth".
(1 Timothy 5:6 KJV)

How come in the presence of God, there are pleasures evermore, fullness of joy, and in fact a promise and direct guarantee of pleasures? "If they obey and serve him, they shall spend their days in prosperity, and their years in pleasures' (Job 36:11-12) and Paul reiterates that God 'giveth us all things to richly to enjoy" (1 Timothy 6:17b). Jesus Christ, the King of the kingdom, enjoins believers to "ask until their joy is FULL."(John 16:24) What then brought about a reversal to the blessedness of God's desires? It's nothing but the fall of man in the Garden of Eden.

> Now we know that what things soever the law saith, it saith to them who are under the law: that every mouth may be stopped, and all the world may become guilty before God. Therefore by the deeds of the law there shall no flesh be justified in his sight: for by the law is the knowledge of sin. For all have sinned, and come short of the glory of God. (Romans 3:19–23)

Herein lies the avenue through which corruption entered into the original blessedness of God toward all creation, and hence perversion of pleasures. Anything enjoyed by God's creature that does not come under the principles of God has the tag of perversion. The reason is that the archenemy of God, Satan, has assumed the God of the principles of this world in all spheres. "In whom the god of this world hath blinded the minds of them which believe not, lest the light of the glorious gospel of Christ, who is the image of God, should shine unto them" (2 Corinthians 4:4 KJV).

Satan, as the god of the systems of this world, paints God as the one who does not want His creatures to have pleasures. Satan turns around to make them have a perverted manner contrary to the Creator's designed way.

Hence, dominion over things initially granted to man turned to domination.

Fellowship with God became doubting God and hiding from Him.

Legitimate pleasures became an act whereby they are gotten illegitimately.

The lust of the flesh took over.

The lust of the eyes took over.

The pride of life took over.

Enmity replaced coexistence.

Friction replaced peace and harmony.

Hatred replaced love and affection.

Avarice replaced generosity.

Selfishness took over from selflessness.

Violence chased peace out of the society.

Death replaced live.

Blessings turned to curses.

Sound health and sound mind turned to malady.

Unity turned to divisions.

Confusion overran orderliness.

On and on, degeneration escalated, and creation has not been the same ever since.

Sanctity of marriage is polluted. System of governance has become a machine of oppression.

Music became the instrument of the devil for diverse perversions.

Entertainment and amusement replaced sobriety, discipline, and decency.

Spiritism replaced spirituality.
Religion took over from righteousness.
Rebellion replaced reverence for God.
Rancor overtook civility.
The rat race replaced teamwork.
Prophet Isaiah lays it out clearly in Isaiah 59:1–15.

> Behold, the Lord's hand is not shortened, that it cannot save; neither his ear heavy that it cannot hear:
>
> But your iniquities have separated between you and your God, and your sins have hid his face from you, that he will not hear.
>
> For your hands are defiled with blood, and your fingers with iniquity; your lips have spoken lies, your tongue hath muttered perverseness.
>
> None calleth for justice, nor any pleadeth for truth: they trust in vanity, and speak lies; they conceive mischief, and bring forth iniquity.
>
> They hatch cockatrice' eggs, and weave the spider's web: he that eateth of their eggs dieth, and that which is crushed breaketh out into a viper.
>
> Their webs shall not become garments, neither shall they cover themselves with their works: their works are works of iniquity, and the act of violence is in their hands.
>
> Their feet run to evil, and they make haste to shed innocent blood: their thoughts are thoughts of iniquity; wasting and destruction are in their paths.

The way of peace they know not; and there is no judgment in their goings: they have made them crooked paths: whosoever goeth therein shall not know peace.

Therefore is judgment far from us, neither doth justice overtake us: we wait for light, but behold obscurity; for brightness, but we walk in darkness.

We grope for the wall like the blind, and we grope as if we had no eyes: we stumble at noon day as in the night; we are in desolate places as dead men.

We roar all like bears, and mourn sore like doves: we look for judgment, but there is none; for salvation, but it is far off from us. For our transgressions are multiplied before thee, and our sins testify against us: for our transgressions are with us; and as for our iniquities, we know them; In transgressing and lying against the Lord, and departing away from our God, speaking oppression and revolt, conceiving and uttering from the heart words of falsehood. And judgment is turned away backward, and justice standeth afar off: for truth is fallen in the street, and equity cannot enter.

Yea, truth faileth; and he that departeth from evil maketh himself a prey: and the Lord saw it, and it displeased him that there was no judgment.

Every institution of God became polluted, bastardized, and perverted, contrary to the original decency and orderliness. The larger the population of things, the bigger the mess.

Human relation was perverted, with no more trust.

Marriage institution was perverted, with no more originality.

Political institution was perverted, with no more rule of law.

Family union was derailed, with no more seeing eye to eye.

Service and worship of God was polluted, with no more sanctity.

Creativity was polluted, replaced with idolatry.

Moderation was trampled under feet to give rise to pride and arrogance.
Lies and deception replaced truth and godliness.
Beauty turned to ashes, and light turned to darkness.
Pleasure in ungodliness swallowed up godly pleasures.
Prophet Hosea confirms what things turned upside down when perverted pleasures took root.

> Hear the word of the Lord, ye children of Israel: for the Lord hath a controversy with the inhabitants of the land, because there is no truth, nor mercy, nor knowledge of God in the land.

> By swearing, and lying, and killing, and stealing, and committing adultery, they break out, and blood toucheth blood. Therefore shall the land mourn, and every one that dwelleth therein shall languish, with the beasts of the field, and with the fowls of heaven; yea, the fishes of the sea also shall be taken away.

> Therefore shall the land mourn, and every one that dwelleth therein shall languish, with the beasts of the field, and with the fowls of heaven; yea, the fishes of the sea also shall be taken away.

> My people are destroyed for lack of knowledge: because thou hast rejected knowledge, I will also reject thee, that thou shalt be no priest to me: seeing thou hast forgotten the law of thy God, I will also forget thy children.

> As they were increased, so they sinned against me: therefore will I change their glory into shame.

> They eat up the sin of my people, and they set their heart on their iniquity.

> For they shall eat, and not have enough: they shall commit whoredom, and shall not increase: because they have left off to take heed to the Lord.

> Whoredom and wine and new wine take away the heart. (Hosea 4:4–11 KJV)

There is no gainsaying the fact that after the fall of Eve and Adam, everything came under a curse, and corruption entered into the hitherto goodly creatures of God. Ever since, there has been perversion of the pleasures originally designed for all. As a result of this, one finds a clear divide between the original and the perverse.

"But she that liveth in pleasure is dead while she liveth" (1 Timothy 5:6 KJV). What type of pleasure? Of course it is perverted pleasure—that is to say, ungodly pleasure. But in the beginning it was not so. Man in the beginning was created in the image of God. He had the thought and mind of God. Hence in Genesis 2:19 it states, "And out of the ground the LORD God formed every beast of the field, and every fowl of the air; and brought them unto Adam to see what he would call them: and whatsoever Adam called every living creature, that was the name thereof."

The fact that God approved of all Adam did was an indication of having the mind of God without contradictions. It's clearly evident that once the mind is polluted, the heart is corrupted, and thereby it affects all other things.

> For a good tree bringeth not forth corrupt fruit; neither doth a corrupt tree bring forth good fruit. For every tree is known by his own fruit. For of thorns men do not gather figs, nor of a bramble bush gather they grapes. A good man out of the good treasure of his heart bringeth forth that which is good; and an evil man out of the evil treasure of his heart bringeth forth that which is evil: for of the abundance of the heart his mouth speaketh. (Luke 6:43–45)

Let's go back to the original. By the way, I had no intention of disrupting the joy, the happiness, the peace of mind, and all the fascinating events built up in your soul and spirit thus far by following the events on the Creator's desire and grand plan. "For I know the thoughts that I think toward you, saith the LORD, thoughts of peace, and not of evil, to give you an expected end" (Jeremiah 29:11).

I know you are saying, if not lamenting, "Why did the plan change?"

I know you wish, just as I do, things continued as originally planned by God, but alas!

I know you wish, just as I do, that there was no Satan to tempt Eve, but alas!

I know you wish, just as I do, that Eve and Adam never failed, but alas!

I know you wish, just as I do, that there was no room for curses in place of blessings, but alas!

I know you wish, just as I do, that varieties of godly pleasures were permanent, but alas!

I know you wish, just as I do that no one had to experience the prevalent lamentations, but alas!

I know you wish, just as I do, all things were as they were in the beginning, but alas!

I know you wish, just as I do, that hell was not a reality, but alas!

However, it's been a dream and not a reality, since the fall of Eve and Adam, to have this experience constantly fulfilled. Therefore it can be said that the original desires of God for all creatures had been elusive under the sun from generation to generation.

However, God has not given up on His original plan.

Since the fall of man, the good pleasures originally designed had been polluted. Even though, according to biblical history, there was a short period after the flood that wiped away the whole earth in the days of Noah, things went back to decay again.

Ten

THE CREATOR'S PATH
TO UTMOST AND
EVERLASTING PLEASURES

God remains God, and His counsel in everything, no matter how long it takes, must stand. He did not abandon His original plan. He made a way to still fulfill His grand desire for all His creatures despite the perversion and pollution that set in. He who began a good thing and put his stamp of approval to be very good designed the best plan to prove that He had created all things for His pleasure. He is the one who opens what no one can shut, and He shuts what no one can open, so He found a way out of love to make a path for an everlasting pleasures for all His creatures by offering Jesus Christ to atone for the sins of the whole world."He that committeth sin is of the devil; for the devil sinneth from the beginning. For this purpose the Son of God was manifested, that he might destroy the works of the devil" (1 John 3:8 KJV).

Jesus Christ, the Son of God, was the only one deemed fit and qualified to redeem the whole of creation to the pleasures of God. All the works of the devil brought about curses, death, vices, sicknesses and afflictions, woes, disappointments, punishments, wars, pains, rebellion, hatred, confusion, and everything evil, culminating in the anger and judgment of God in Romans 1:18, "For the wrath of God is revealed from heaven against all ungodliness and unrighteousness of men, who hold the truth in unrighteousness." This eventually leads to everlasting punishment in hellfire for everyone who does not take advantage of the prescription of God for pardon through faith in the sacrifice of Jesus Christ on the cross for atonement for all sins. "And he is the propitiation for our sins: and not for ours only, but also for the sins of the whole world" (1 John 2:2 KJV).

Apostle Peter clarifies further that whosoever does not want to incur the wrath of God but desires to have the everlasting pleasures of God has no other choice but to believe the good news of redemption though repentance from sins, forsaking of the sins, and believing in Jesus Christ as the only Lord and Savior. Acts 4:12 states, "Neither is there salvation in any other: for there is none other name under heaven given among men, whereby we must be saved."

The implication of redemption through Jesus Christ is the only guarantee from God, the Creator, to live in everlasting pleasures in heaven with God. John 3:16 (KJV) says, "For God so loved the world, that he gave his only begotten Son, that whosoever believeth in him should not perish, but have everlasting life." Jesus Christ made the promise of eternal bliss, eternal glory, internal joy, eternal peace, eternal blessedness, and eternal possessions for all who believe in him, and their lives are transformed before death.

> Let not your heart be troubled: ye believe in God, believe also in me. In my Father's house are many mansions: if it were not so, I would have told you. I go to prepare a place for you. And if I go and prepare a place for you, I will come again, and receive you unto myself; that where I am, there ye may be also. (John 14:2–3 KJV)

Here lies the crux of the matter with respect to the destiny of God's creation. It goes without saying that all that God created was for pleasures from the onset. That design had an obstruction and got corrupted through the temptation from Satan, and Adam and Eve fell, thereby incurring the wrath and displeasure of God. Things have never been the same since. There has never been a permanent, continuous, widespread blessedness as it was in the Garden of Eden before the fall. The final solution emerged from God through His only begotten Son to redeem all things to God's designed pleasures, whereby there will be a creation of a new heaven and a new earth. "And whosoever was not found written in the book of life was cast into the lake of fire" (Revelation 20:15).

In other words, only those who accept the offer of God by accepting Jesus Christ as their personal Lord and Savior will have the privilege of enjoying the pleasures of God forever in heaven. Those who reject will be punished and will miss the opportunity forever. There shall be lamentation in hellfire.

> Jesus answered and said unto Nicodemus, a man who wanted to know how to enter into God's everlasting and pleasurable life. "Verily, verily, I say unto thee, except a man be born again, he cannot see the kingdom of God." (John 3:16–17)

There are only two options from the Creator to humankind to choose from regarding eternal destinations before death: Heaven, the place designed for everlasting pleasures for all the inhabitants, or hell, a place of everlasting torment. "And if thy foot offend thee, cut it off: it is better for thee to enter halt into life, than having two feet to be cast into hell, into the fire that never shall be quenched: Where their worm dieth not, and the fire is not quenched" (Mark 9:45–46). To have the utmost pleasures of God for which God, the Creator, designed all things, the decision is the most critical decision in one's lifetime.

It is clear from generation to generation that no one finds pleasures in pains, anguish, sicknesses and afflictions, rejections, sorrows, and unspeakable sufferings. Even those who seem to have things going well for them on Earth are not free from one trauma or another, one tragedy or another, one devastation at some point in time, one loss or another. Even the best they might have or possess is subject to insecurity and constant challenges. It is also significant to note that all the experiences of pleasures in this present world have their ups and downs.

None is absolutely satisfactory.

None is absolutely pleasurable before, during, and after.

None is realistically all-around pleasurable.

None is everlasting, but short-lived.

None is as stable as desired.

None is absolutely comfortable.

None is perfect in the real sense of the word.

None is perfectly harmonized with others.

All are conditional.

All are subject to decay.

All are subject to faults.

All are subject to the law of diminishing returns.

Pleasures of this world are transient.

Most of the pleasures of this world are subjective.

Most of the pleasures of this world are gotten at the expense of others.

Pleasures of this world are minimal due to negative environmental circumstances.

They are not usually sustainable.

They are subject to weariness and labor.

They are usually not dependable or durable.

They are subject to corruption and manipulations.

They are at the expense of other factors.

They are subject to change with time and seasons.

They are not substantial enough.

The reason is that "all have sinned, and come short of the glory of God" (Romans 3:23 KJV). The entire creation was meant to show forth the glory of God to satisfying the pleasures of the Creator, but because the glory had departed with the fall of man, it behooves on God to do a new thing. The glory of God in its fullness will be restored only at the advent of a new heaven and a new Earth. Though there will be a taste of this during the thousand years of the reign of Christ on Earth, even that will be limited in comparison to the period when all things are made new.

God has given only two options to humans, whom He initially

created in His image: to willingly surrender to Christ as Lord and savior before death and receive everlasting life in heaven thereafter as a reward, or to be damned and doomed forever in hellfire with the devil and his angels.

> Enter ye in at the strait gate: for wide is the gate, and broad is the way, that leadeth to destruction, and many there be which go in thereat: Because strait is the gate, and narrow is the way, which leadeth unto life, and few there be that find it. Matthew 7:13–14 (KJV)

Those who are willing and obedient shall inherit all things.

Eleven

───── ✄ ─────

WHAT, THEN, IS AT STAKE?

There is a statement of fact that everyone desires to have pleasure in all areas of life. Who does not love to have fullness of love?

Who does not want satisfaction in life?
Who does not want to be happy in life?
Who does not want to be fulfilled in life?
Who does not want to have fullness of joy?
Who does not want to be surrounded with good things of life?
Who desires poverty?
Who desires wretchedness?
Who desires failures?
Who desires sicknesses and afflictions?
Who desires to be oppressed or suppressed?
Who wants pains, anguish, and punishments?
Who wishes for curses rather than blessings?
Who wishes for penury rather than riches?
Who would rather be in bondage rather than be free?
Who prefers sorrow instead of joy?
Who prefers heaviness of heart instead of laughter?
Who prefers wars to peace?
Who prefers disasters and sadness to happiness?
Who prefers mourning to dancing?

Who prays for tears and sighs?
Who prays for hardship?
Who prays for losses?
Who prays for nightmares?
Who prays for downfalls?
Who prays for fire and brimstone?
Who prays to spend eternity in hellfire?

At this juncture, it should be pointed out without mincing words that the very reason we want to go to heaven is for God's pleasures. Everything in heaven is pleasurable. That is the long and short story of the designs of God.

What does a Christian need the streets of gold for?
What does he need the mansions in heaven for?
What does he need fellowship for?
What does he need rest for?
What does he need peace for?
What does he need love for?
What does he need singing for?
What does he need rewards for?
What does he need an everlasting life of joy for?
Why does he strive to avoid hell at all cost?
One simple reason is that there is no single pleasure in hell.
There is anguish and suffering in hell.
There is no sleep, day or night, in hell.
There is fire and burning without end in hell.
There is no single comfort in hell.
There is no singing or rejoicing in hell.
There is no single day of laughter in hell.
There is no single day of fellowship in hell.
There is no single day of peace in hell.
There is no drop of water to drink in hell, though there shall be thirst.
There is no love in hell.

There is no food in hell, though there shall be hunger.
There is no light in hell.
There is no relief but everlasting pain and torment in hell.
Little wonder that Jesus sternly warned everyone,

> And if thy hand offend thee, cut it off: it is better for thee to enter into life maimed, than having two hands to go into hell, into the fire that never shall be quenched: Where their worm dieth not, and the fire is not quenched. And if thy foot offend thee, cut it off: it is better for thee to enter halt into life, than having two feet to be cast into hell, into the fire that never shall be quenched: Where their worm dieth not, and the fire is not quenched. And if thine eye offend thee, pluck it out: it is better for thee to enter into the kingdom of God with one eye, than having two eyes to be cast into hell fire: 48Where their worm dieth not, and the fire is not quenched. (Mark 9:43–48)

The summary of hell is therefore a place without God and the place of fullness of His displeasure. Heaven is the direct opposite: a place with God and the fullness of His pleasures. The Earth in the original state was meant to be an extension of heaven before sin entered in. Everyone since Adam and until the end of the world will eventually end up in either of these two destinations. Heaven or hell? It's up to each individual to make a choice as to where to spend eternity.

There are only two groups of people in the world.

Saints or sinners.
Redeemed or reprobates.
Justified or judged.
Saved or shackled.
Heaven bound or hell bound.
Free or fettered.

In the light of the aforementioned final destinations of all humans, I join the generals who left their footprints on the sand of life in their ministries and devotion to the cause of God to appeal to all readers of this book

Moses–

> I call heaven and earth to record this day against you, that I have set before you life and death, blessing and cursing: therefore choose life that both thou and thy seed may live. (Deuteronomy 30:19)

Ezekiel

> The soul that sinneth, it shall die. The son shall not bear the iniquity of the father, neither shall the father bear the iniquity of the son: the righteousness of the righteous shall be upon him, and the wickedness of the wicked shall be upon him. But if the wicked will turn from all his sins that he hath committed, and keep all my statutes, and do that which is lawful and right, he shall surely live, he shall not die. All his transgressions that he hath committed, they shall not be mentioned unto him: in his righteousness that he hath done he shall live. Have I any pleasure at all that the wicked should die? saith the Lord God: and not that he should return from his ways, and live? (Ezekiel 18–23)

> Say unto them, As I live, saith the Lord GOD, I have no pleasure in the death of the wicked; but that the wicked turn from his way and live: turn ye, turn ye from your evil ways; for why will ye die, O house of Israel? (Ezekiel 33:11)

Isaiah

Come now, and let us reason together, saith the Lord: though your sins be as scarlet, they shall be as white as snow; though they be red like crimson, they shall be as wool. (Isaiah 1:18)

Paul

Knowing therefore the terror of the Lord, we persuade men. (2Corinthians 5:11)

Jesus Christ

Come unto me, all ye that labor and are heavy laden, and I will give you rest. (Matthew 11:28 KJV)

Conclusion

If you desire an abundant, endless life and not everlasting burnings;

If you want to have everlasting pleasures and not everlasting pains;

If you want to enjoy life in its fullness and not fullness of sorrows;

If you love yourself and want to experience the purest of it forever, and not the reverse;

If you crave for goodness and mercies for all eternity, and not horrors and nightmare;

If you want to live forever with a loving God, and not with dreadful Satan and demons;

If you want to see light you never saw before instead of perpetual darkness for all eternity;

If you want to have life in the most indescribably beautiful environment forever and not in hell;

If you want satisfaction beyond your wildest imaginations instead of everlasting horrors;

If you care to have glory of the highest nature rather than everlasting shame and regrets;

If you'll rather have peace and rest rather than turmoil and perpetual discomfort;

If you will prefer the pleasures of God rather than His fury and displeasure;

If you want to experience what eyes have not seen, what ears of not heard, and what beats the imaginations of the finest minds that God has prepared for those who love Him;

Then choose Christ, choose the Creator of heaven and earth.

For he saith, I have heard thee in a time accepted, and in the day of salvation have I succored thee: behold, now is the accepted time; behold, now is the day of salvation. (2 Corinthians 6:2)

You can then experience the good and loving God and can chorus with those who will live with him forever in heaven.

Thou art worthy, O Lord, to receive glory and honor and power: for thou hast created all things, and for thy pleasure they are and were created.(Revelation 4:11)

Bibliography

"Taking Care of People: Benefits of Fruits." https://health-care-clinic. org/fruits/index.htm.

Half Your Plate. "Fruits and Veggies." https://www.halfyourplate.ca/ fruits-and-veggies/veggies-a-z.

Wikipedia. "Complete Metamorphosis." Updated June, 12, 2020. *https://en.wikipedia.org/wiki/Holometabolism.*

Wikipedia. "Hanging gardens of Babylon" Wikipedia.Updated November,27,2020https://en.wikipedia.org/wiki/Hanging_Gardens_ of_Babylon

World's Most Awesome. "Fastest Animals in the World—Top 12." Updated February 15, 2019. https://www.worldsmostawesome.com/ lists/fastest-animals-in-the-world-top-12.

Chuck. "Characteristics of Formal Gardens." Karen's Garden Tips. February 9, 2012. http://www.karensgardentips.com/garden-design-2/ characteristics-of-formal-gardens.

The Mysterious World. "Top 10 Most Beautiful Birds in the World." https://themysteriousworld.com/most-beautiful-birds-in-the-world.

The Mysterious World. "Top 10 Most Beautiful Birds in the World." https://themysteriousworld.com/most-beautiful-birds-in-the-world.

Printed in the United States
By Bookmasters